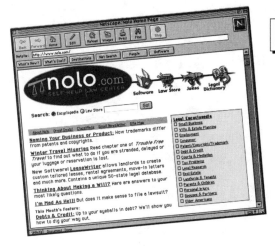

FIRST EDITION

Nolo's California

Quick Corp™

Incorporate your business
without a lawyer

BY ATTORNEY ANTHONY MANCUSO

NOLO PRESS BERKELEY

Your Responsibility When Using a Self-Help Law Book

We've done our best to give you useful and accurate information in this book. But laws and procedures change frequently and are subject to differing interpretations. If you want legal advice backed by a guarantee, see a lawyer. If you use this book, it's your responsibility to make sure that the facts and general advice contained in it are applicable to your situation.

Keeping Up-to-Date

To keep its books up to date, Nolo Press issues new printings and new editions periodically. New printings reflect minor legal changes and technical corrections. New editions contain major legal changes, major text additions or major reorganizations. To find out if a later printing or edition of any Nolo book is available, call Nolo Press at 510-549-1976 or check our Website at www.nolo.com.

To stay current, follow the "Update" service at our Website: www.nolo.com. In another effort to help you use Nolo's latest materials, we offer a 25% discount off the purchase of the new edition of your Nolo book when you turn in the cover of an earlier edition. (See the "Special Upgrade Offer" in the back of the book.)

FIRST EDITION	April 1999
EDITOR	Beth Laurence
ILLUSTRATIONS	Mari Stein
COVER DESIGN	Toni Ihara
BOOK DESIGN	Jackie Mancuso
PROOFREADER	Robert Wells
INDEX	Thérèse Shere
PRINTING	Custom Printing Company

Mancuso, Anthony.
    Nolo's California quick corp : incorporate your business without a
lawyer / by Anthony Mancuso.
        p.   cm.
    Includes index.
    ISBN 0-87337-477-0
    1. Incorporation--California--Popular works.   I. Title.
KFC345.Z9M26 1999
   346.794'06622--dc21   99-12534
                                      CIP

Quantity sales: For information on bulk purchases or corporate premium sales, please contact the Special Sales department. For academic sales or textbook adoptions, ask for Academic Sales. 800-955-4775, Nolo Press, Inc., 950 Parker St., Berkeley, CA, 94710.

Acknowledgements

Special thanks to Beth Laurence for editing and tightening up the information in this book. Also to Toni Ihara for production and design, and to Mari Stein for her imaginative illustrations. A heartfelt thanks to the hardworking people at Nolo Press for their help in making it all happen.

CONTENTS

Introduction

CHAPTER 1
Overview of California Corporations

CHAPTER 2
Choose a Corporate Name

CHAPTER 3
File Articles of Incorporation

Prepare Corporate Bylaws

Prepare Minutes of First Board Meeting

Issue Shares of Stock

Finding Helpful Lawyers and Accountants

Incorporation Forms

INTRODUCTION

This book is meant to help entrepreneurs form a California corporation on their own, with little effort and expense. It is intended for those who have already decided that the corporate form is the best legal structure for conducting business. With this in mind, in Chapter 1 we provide a general overview—not a comprehensive treatment—of the primary characteristics of the corporate form, while covering the basic requirements of forming a California business corporation—one that is formed to transact one or more types of profit-making businesses. From Chapter 2 on, we get right into the nuts and bolts of preparing the legal paperwork to form a California corporation.

This book shows you how to prepare the legal documents necessary to form a California corporation. These include:

- Articles of Incorporation (filed with California Secretary of State)
- Bylaws
- Minutes of First Meeting of Board of Directors
- Notice of Stock Issuance (filed with California Department of Corporations)
- Stock Certificates
- Receipts and Bills of Sale (to document payment for initial shares).

These legal forms are provided as tear-out documents in the Appendix of this book, which can be filled in with a typewriter.

ELECTRONIC FORMS AVAILABLE FOR COMPUTER USERS

If you prefer to use your computer to complete the legal forms included in the Appendix of this book, you can purchase and download electronic versions of these forms from the Nolo Press Website. Point your browser to http://www.nolo.com/item/qinc_forms.html for detailed purchase information.

 FOR ADDITIONAL INFORMATION ON FORMING A CALIFORNIA CORPORATION:

- For a fuller treatment of the legal and tax characteristics of the corporate form, and a comparison to other types of business entities such as sole proprietorships, partnerships, limited liability companies, see *How to Form Your Own California Corporation,* by Anthony Mancuso (Nolo Press).

OTHER NOLO CORPORATE RESOURCES

- *The Corporate Minutes Book: A Legal Guide to Taking Care of Corporate Business,* by Anthony Mancuso, shows you how to prepare standard minutes of annual and special director and shareholder meetings for an existing corporation. It also contains resolutions to approve the various legal, tax, financial and business transactions that commonly occur during the life of a small corporation. All forms and resolutions are provided as tear-outs and forms on disk.

- *The California Professional Corporation Handbook,* by Anthony Mancuso, shows professionals, such as doctors and other healthcare professionals, lawyers, accountants, architects and others how to limit their personal liability for business debts by forming a professional corporation. Complete with tear-out forms and forms on disk. Appendices include the special incorporation rules for each profession.

- *How to Create a Buy-Sell Agreement and Control the Destiny of Your Small Business*, by Bethany Laurence and Anthony Mancuso. This national title contains step-by-step instructions and forms to prepare a buy-sell agreement for a small business corporation. The purpose of a buy-sell agreement is to help shareholders and other business owners keep ownership of a small business in the hands of the founders, and to settle the thorny issues of how to buy back shares from departing or deceased owners or their spouses, estates and heirs. The critical issue of how shares of a small, privately held business should be valued when they are bought back by the business or the remaining owners is also explained in this important book. In short, the adoption of a buy-sell agreement is a must for any closely held corporation.

Using Professionals to Help You Incorporate

Lawyers can charge up to $2,000 or even more to incorporate your business. To allow you to save money and spend it more usefully elsewhere, this book shows you how to fill in standard incorporation forms. Again, it's not hard, and the investment of your time and energy should be modest. But although not required by law, we do think that it can make sense to consult an attorney to check over your incorporation papers, particularly if you have special questions or needs—for example, if you want to implement a complicated stock structure. And, of course, you may have corporate tax questions, which you will want to discuss with a tax advisor. To help you find the right person to answer legal and tax questions, we discuss how to locate a helpful lawyer and tax advisor in Chapter 7.

ICONS

Throughout this book, these icons alert you to certain information.

 Fast Track

We use this icon to let you know when you may skip information that may not be relevant to your situation.

 Warning

This icon alerts you potential problems.

 Recommended Reading

When you see this icon, a list of additional resources that can assist you follows.

 Tip

A legal or commonsense tip to help you understand or comply with legal requirements.

e-Form

Refers to electronic forms that are available for purchase and download from http://www.nolo.com

■.

Overview of California Corporations

In this chapter we review the main characteristics of the corporate business form that make it attractive and unique as a business structure, as well as the rules and requirements you'll need to understand in order to form your corporation.

A. Corporate Characteristics

Many entrepreneurs and business owners choose the corporate form because of its built-in organizational structure, its unique access to investment sources and the protection from personal liability that it provides to its owners.

1. The Separate Corporate "Person"

What sets the corporation apart, in a theoretical sense, from all other types of businesses is that it is a legal entity separate from the people who own, control, manage or operate it. Corporate and tax statutes view the corporation as a legal "person," capable of entering into contracts, incurring debts and paying taxes separately from its owners. In the following sections, we look at the special corporate characteristics that result from treating the corporation as a separate legal and tax "person."

2. Perpetual Existence

The separate corporate person is, in some senses, immortal. Unlike a sole proprietorship, partnership or LLC, which can sometimes terminate upon the death or withdrawal of the owners, a corporation has an independent legal existence that continues despite changeovers in management or ownership. Of course, like any business, a corporation can be terminated by the mutual consent of the owners for personal or economic reasons and, in some cases, involuntarily, as in corporate bankruptcy proceedings. Nonetheless, the fact that a corporation does not depend for its legal existence on a particular individual's life or continuing ownership does positively influence creditors, employees and others who participate in the operations of the business. This is particularly true as the business grows.

3. Limited Personal Liability for Business Debts

As a general rule, the corporate "person," not the owners of a corporation (called shareholders), is solely liable for the corporation's debts, claims and other liabilities (lawsuits, fines, penalties and the like). Put another way, this means that a person who invests in a corporation (a shareholder) normally only stands to lose the amount of money or the value of the property that he has paid for its stock. As a result, if the corporation for some reason (bad luck or mismanagement, for example) cannot pay its debts or other financial obligations, creditors can take control of the business's assets, but cannot seize or sell the shareholder's home, car or other personal assets.

Example: Rackafrax Dry Cleaners, Inc., a California corporation, has several bad years in a row. When it finally files for bankruptcy, Rackafrax owes $50,000 to a number of suppliers and $80,000 as a result of a lawsuit, for uninsured losses stemming from a fire. Stock in Rackafrax is owned by Harry Rack, Edith Frax and John Quincy Taft. Fortunately (for the shareholders), Rackafrax's creditors cannot go after their personal assets to get the money Rackafrax owes; only Rackafrax's corporate assets are subject to these liabilities.

Comparison to Other Business Forms: Unlike corporate shareholders, the owners of a sole proprietorship and the general partners in a partnership are *personally* liable for all business debts and claims—creditors can take their houses, cars and personal assets for unpaid business debts. Like corporate shareholders, the limited partners in a limited partnership, and all owners of an LLC (called members), are not personally liable for business liabilities.

a. Exceptions to the Rule of Personal Liability Protection

In some situations, corporate directors, officers and shareholders of a corporation *can* be held responsible for paying the debts owed by their corporation. Here are the most common exceptions to the rule of limited personal liability (these exceptions below also apply to other limited liability business forms, such as the LLC):

Personal Guarantees. Often when a bank or other creditor lends money to a small corporation, particularly a newly formed one, it requires that the people who own the corporation agree to repay the debt from their personal assets should the corporation default on the loan; shareholders may even have to pledge equity in a house or other personal assets as security for repayment of the debt. Of course, shareholders can just say no (and not personally guarantee any debts), but if they do, their corporation may not qualify for needed loans.

Federal and State Taxes. If a corporation fails to pay income or payroll taxes, the IRS and the California Franchise Tax Board are likely to attempt to recover the unpaid taxes from "responsible employees" of the corporation—a category that often includes the directors, officers and shareholders of a small corporation.

Unlawful or Unauthorized Transactions. If one or more shareholders use the corporation to defraud third parties, or if they deliberately make a decision (or fail to make one) that results in physical harm to others or others' property (because of the failure to maintain premises properly, the manufacture of unsafe products or environmental pollution, for example), a court may "pierce the corporate veil" and hold the shareholders of a small corporation personally liable for damages (monetary losses) caused to others, or for fines and penalties resulting from wrongful or unlawful corporate behavior.

Fortunately, most of the problem areas where shareholders might be held personally liable for corporate obligations can be avoided by following a few commonsense principles (principles you'll probably adhere to anyway). First, don't do anything dishonest or illegal. Second, make sure your corporation does the same, by having it obtain any necessary permits, licenses or clearances for its business operations, and by making sure it obeys all local, state and federal regulations. Third, withhold and pay corporate income and payroll taxes on time. Fourth, don't personally obligate yourself to repay corporate debts or obligations unless you fully understand and accept the consequences. Fifth, act like a corporation—that is, follow corporate procedures such as issuing shares, holding shareholder and board meetings and recording management decisions in the corporate minutes.

b. Some California Professionals Must Form a Professional Corporation

A business corporation—the type you can form with this book—does not have the power to engage in the practice of certain professions that involve a special professional-client relationship. The theory behind this rule is that the corporate entity should not come between the special relationship between the professional and the person receiving her services. If a professional practice of this type is incorporated, it must form a special type of corporation, called a "professional corporation," and comply with special state incorporation formalities. The following is a list of professionals who cannot form regular business corporations:

Accountant [1]
Acupuncturist
Architect [1, 2]

Attorney [1]
Audiologist
Chiropractor
Clinical Social Worker
Dentist
Doctor (medical doctors including surgeons)
Marriage, Family and Child Counselor
Nurse
Optometrist
Osteopath (physician or surgeon)
Pharmacist
Physical Therapist
Physician's Assistant
Podiatrist
Psychologist
Shorthand Reporter
Speech Pathologist
Veterinarian. [2]

[1] As an alternative to forming a professional corporation, accountants, architects and lawyers can limit their personal liability for the business debts of their professional practice by forming a California registered limited liability partnership (RLLP). This RLLP structure, like the professional corporation, limits each professional's personal liability for the regular commercial debts of the practice. The other common limited liability business form—the limited liability company—is currently not available to California professionals. But this law may change. For more information on the special rules for business formation that affect your profession, call your state licensing board.

[2] Architects and veterinarians have the option to incorporate as professional corporations or as regular business corporations (the latter is the type of corporation this book shows you how to form). Typically, to avoid extra formalities and operating restrictions associated with the professional corporation, architects and veterinarians often choose to incorporate as regular business corporations. If you decide to use this book to form your architecture or veterinary business corporation, first check with your state board in Sacramento to make sure this information is current—that is, that you currently have the option to form a regular business corporation instead of a professional corporation.

MALPRACTICE: ATTENTION DOCTORS, LAWYERS AND ACCOUNTANTS

No matter which business form a doctor, lawyer or accountant uses (professional corporation or registered limited liability partnership), he remains personally liable for his own malpractice and the malpractice of other professionals in the firm under his supervision. A professional corporation or RLLP can at least limit the members' liability for regular business debts.

4. Corporate People

While a corporation is a legal "person" capable of making contracts, paying taxes and asserting its own legal identity in court, it needs real people to carry out its business. In fact, perhaps the most unique benefit of forming a corporation is the ability to distribute ownership, management and executive decision-making duties to the various corporate people. Unlike partnerships and LLCs, the corporate structure comes ready-made with a built-in, legal separation of these three activity levels, each with its own legal authority, rules, and ability to participate in corporate income and profits. The corporate people are classified as:

- **Incorporators**—the person or persons who form the corporation by signing Articles of Incorporation and filing them with the California Secretary of State; in practical terms, the founders of the corporation.
- **Shareholders**—the persons or entities that own a percentage of the assets of the corporation in the form of "stock," or "shares"; in other words, the owners of the corporation.
- **Directors**—one or more persons who serve on the corporation's board of directors and manage the corporation—the overseers of the company. Under California law, a business corporation must have at least three directors if the corporation has three or more shareholders. However, a corporation with two shareholders is allowed to have only two directors, and a corporation with only one shareholder is allowed to have one or two directors.

Directors do not have to be shareholders of the corporation, although in many small corporations they will be.

- **Officers**—the person or persons who fill the positions of President, Vice President, Secretary and Treasurer—the executives of the corporation. More than one, or even all of the offices, may be filled by the same individual. (Like directors, officers do not have to be shareholders of the corporation, though in many small corporations they will be.)

California does not impose age, residency or other requirements on any corporate person (incorporator, director, officer or shareholder). However, in order to avoid contractual problems, we assume your incorporators, directors and officers will be at least 18 years of age.

ONE-PERSON CORPORATION ALLOWED:

The state of California allows you to form a one-person corporation with you as your corporation's only incorporator, shareholder, director and officer.

Rather than burdening the business with unnecessary levels of authority, the built-in formality of corporations, usually provides unique opportunities for structuring your business.

Example 1: *Myra, Danielle and Rocco form their own three-person corporation, Skate City, Incorporated, a skate and bike shop in Venice Beach, Los Angeles. Storefront access to the Venice Beach rollerblading and bike path makes it popular with local rollerbladers and bicyclists. Needing more cash, the three incorporators approach their relatives for investment capital. Rocco's brother, Tony, and Danielle's sister, Collette, each chip in $10,000 in return for shares in the business. Myra's Aunt Kate lends the corporation $25,000 in return for an interest-only promissory note, with the principal amount to be repaid at the end of five years. Here's how they break down the management, executive and financial structure of the corporation:*

Shareholders: There are five shareholders: the three founders, Myra, Danielle and Rocco, and the two investors, Tony and Collette. (Aunt Kate is only a creditor of the corporation, not a shareholder.)

Board of Directors: *The management team, which meets regularly to analyze and project financial performance and review store operations, consists of the three founders, Myra, Danielle and Rocco, and one of the other three investors. This fourth investor board position is a one-year rotating seat. For the first year Tony has the investor board seat; the next year, Collette, the third year, Aunt Kate; this pattern repeats every three years. The directors have one vote apiece, regardless of share ownership—this means the three founders can outvote the investor vote on the board, but this also ensures that each of the investors periodically gets to hear board discussions and has a say in major management decisions.*

Executive Team: The three founders also make themselves the officers, or executive team, of the corporation. They are charged with overseeing day-to-day business, supervising employees, keeping track of ordering, inventory and sales activities, and generally putting into practice the goals set by the board. Myra is the President, and Danielle the Vice President. Rocco fills the remaining officer positions of Secretary/Treasurer of the corporation, but he really only performs part-time administrative tasks. Rocco's real vocation—or avocation—is training to be a professional rollerblader, and he hopes someday to have his own corporate sponsor (maybe Skate City if profits continue to roll in).

Participation in Profits: *Corporate net profits, for the time being, are used to stock inventory, pay rent on the Venice Beach storefront and pay all the other usual and customary expenses of doing business. The two full-time executives, Myra and Danielle, get a corporate salary, plus a year-end bonus when profits are good. Rocco gets a small stipend (hourly pay) for his part-time work. Otherwise, he and the two investor-shareholders (Tony and Collette) are simply sitting on their shares, since Skate City is not yet in a position to pay dividends—all excess profits of the corporation are used to expand the store's product lines and to add a new service facility at the back of the store. But even if dividends are never paid, all three know that their stock will be worth a good deal if the business is successful. Hopefully, they'll be able to cash in their shares if the business sells or if they decide to sell their shares back to the corporation (or, who knows, if Skate City goes public someday by making a direct public offer-*

ing of shares to customers, friends and other family members). Aunt Kate, the most conservative member of the investment group, will look to ongoing interest payments as her share in corporate profits, and will get her capital back when the principal amount of her loan is repaid.

What's the point of this example? Simply, that the mechanisms to put this custom-tailored investment, management and executive structure into place are built into the Skate City corporation. To erect it, all that is needed is to fill in a few blanks on standard incorporation forms (and to prepare a standard promissory note for Aunt Kate). To duplicate this structure as a partnership or LLC would require a specially drafted partnership or LLC operating agreement with custom language and plenty of review by the founders and the investment group (and, no doubt, their lawyers). The corporate business structure is designed to handle this division of investment, management and day-to-day responsibilities with a minimum of extra time, trouble and expense.

The fact that there are legal differences in the rights and responsibilities of shareholders, directors and officers becomes particularly attractive as a business grows and people from outside the initial circle of founders become involved in the business (as investors, lenders or even public shareholders).

Example 2: Leila runs a lunch-counter business that provides her both a decent income and an escape from the cubicled office environment in which she was once unhappily ensconced. Business has been slow, but Leila has a new idea that will give the business more appeal, as well as make it more fun for her. She changes the decor to reflect a tropical motif, installs a saltwater aquarium facing the lunch counter, adds coral-reef (metal halide) lighting and light-reflective wall paneling, and renames the business the "Tide Pool." Leila augments the standard lunch-counter fare with a special bouillabaisse soup entrée and a selection of organic salads and fruit-juice drinks, and adds a seafood and sushi dinner menu to cater to the after-work crowd. Leila has her hands full, doing most of the remodeling work herself and preparing the expanded menu each day.

The new operation enjoys great success, and a newspaper in the nearby capital city features the Tide Pool in an article on trendy eating spots, giving it a rave review. Patronage increases and Leila hires a cook and adds three waiters to help her.

Then a local entrepreneur, Sally, asks Leila if she would be interested in franchising other Tide Pools throughout the country. Sally, the entrepreneur, finds an investment group that will help develop a franchise plan plus fund the new operation. She asks Leila to travel nationally to help set up franchise operations for the first year, and to take on a managerial role and substantial stake in the new venture.

Leila likes the idea—sure, she'll have to get back into the work-a-day world, but on her own terms, as a consultant and business owner. Besides, she's feeling overworked managing the Tide Pool by herself, and it would be a relief to have the new venture take over the business. The investment group wants a managerial role in the franchise operation, plus a comprehensive set of financial controls. Leila and the investment group agree to incorporate the new venture as "Tide Pool Franchising, Inc."

The corporate business structure is a good fit. Leila will assume a managerial role as a director of the new company, along with Sally and a member of the venture capital firm. The new firm hires two seasoned small business people, one as President and one as Chief Financial Officer/Secretary, to run the new franchise operation. Business begins with the original Tide Pool as the first franchise location, and Leila gets started working for a good salary, plus commission, setting up other franchise locations.

If the new venture makes a go of it, Leila and the investment group might be able to either sell their shares back to the corporation at a healthy profit, or, if growth is substantial and consistent, take the company public in a few years, selling their stock in the corporation at a sizable profit once a market has been established for the corporation's publicly held shares.

THE CALIFORNIA CLOSE CORPORATION—SPECIAL REQUIREMENTS AND CHARACTERISTICS

A California for-profit corporation with 35 or fewer shareholders may, by including special "close corporation" provisions in its Articles of Incorporation and on its stock certificates, elect to be organized as a California close corporation. Technically, California close corporations are referred to as "statutory close corporations" to distinguish them from "closely held corporations." The latter type of corporation is not specifically mentioned in the California statutes—it loosely means any privately held corporation owned and operated by a few business associates, friends and/or family members—that is, the type of corporation most readers will wish to form.

The main reason for forming a statutory close corporation is to be allowed to operate the corporation under the terms of a close-corporation shareholders' agreement, which can provide for informal management of the corporation and allow the corporate entity to operate under partnership-type rules. For example, a close-corporation shareholders' agreement can dispense with the need for annual director or shareholder meetings, corporate officers, or even the board of directors itself, allowing the shareholders to manage and carry out the business of the corporation without having to put on their director or officer hats. And, as with a partnership, profits can be distributed without regard to stock ownership, meaning that a 10% shareholder could, for example, receive 25% of the profits (dividends). In effect, a close corporation can waive many of the statutory rules that apply to regular California for-profit corporations and can establish its own operating procedures according to the terms of its close-corporation shareholders' agreement.

Most incorporators do not choose to form close corporations, however. There are a number of reasons for their lack of popularity. To begin with, most corporations do not need, or wish, to operate their corporation under informal or nonstandard close-corporation shareholder agreement rules and procedures. In fact, many incorporators form a corporation in order to rely on the traditional corporation and tax statutes that apply to regular profit corporations. (We discuss corporate taxation in Section B, below). Secondly, shares of stock in a close corporation contain built-in (automatic) restrictions on transferability, and most incorporators do not want their shares to contain these transfer restrictions. Please see a lawyer if you are interested in forming this special type of California corporation—the forms in this book cannot be used to form a statutory close corporation.

5. Raising Capital: Selling Shares and Taking Out Loans

Continuing with our corporate person metaphor: you must supply your corporation with capital in order to feed the new corporate person.

HOW MUCH CAPITAL SHOULD YOU RAISE?

There is no minimum capitalization requirement for corporations in California—that is, you can start a California corporation with next to no money, property or other assets. But, even though there are no minimum capitalization requirements, it's important to pay adequate capital into your corporation. To give yourself the best chance of making a success of your corporation, and to avoid unnecessary legal problems, pay into your corporation enough money (and/or assets) to commence operations and cover at least foreseeable short-range taxes, expenses and potential liabilities likely to occur in your particular business. If you don't, under certain circumstances, if a corporation can't pay its debts, a court may conclude that the corporation was undercapitalized, and used as a device to deceive or defraud creditors. The court can hold corporate principals personally liable for the corporation's unpaid debts or liabilities—in other words, "pierce the corporate veil" of the corporation, as we discussed in Section A3a above.

To start your corporation, you may need more money than you (and your co-owners, if you have them) can muster from your own savings. Fortunately, corporations offer a terrific structure for raising money from friends, family and business associates—by selling them shares in your corporation. There is something special about stock ownership, even in a small business, that attracts others. People like to receive the decorative pieces of paper that are handed out as stock certificates, and enjoy being part-owners of a business without having to risk personal liability. (In Section C, below, we'll talk about how to offer your shares for sale to your family and others while complying with the law.)

Shareholders must pay some consideration (money or property) for shares (even if you'll be the sole owner and shareholder), but there is no statutory requirement as to how much is necessary. There are several ways shareholders can pay for shares in your new corporation. In California, corporate shares of stock may be sold for:

- cash
- tangible or intangible property received by the corporation prior to the stock issuance
- labor or services actually rendered the corporation prior to the stock issuance, and/or
- the cancellation of a debt owed by the corporation to the person receiving the shares.

If shares are sold for consideration (a payment) other than cash, the board of directors must state in a resolution the fair value of the services, property or other form of payment paid for the shares (that is, they must state a dollar amount that represents the payment's fair market value). We cover this resolution in the minutes of Chapter 5, Section A.

Note that shares in a California corporation cannot be sold in return for a promissory note from the purchaser (in which the shareholder promises to pay for the shares after the stock issuance) unless the note is secured by collateral other than the shares themselves. Also, stock cannot be sold in return for a promise from a shareholder to perform services for the corporation *in the future* (unless the stock is sold as part of a stock purchase or option plan for employees or directors).

Example: Thomas and Richard, after a bit of brainstorming, decide to form a Beverly Hills hang-gliding tour service, called "Two Sheets in the Wind, Inc." Unfortunately, they know only one person who would be willing to actually strap himself in as their tour guide, a fellow flying enthusiast, Harold. Harold sees the unique possibilities associated with this enterprise and insists on owning shares in the corporation rather than being a mere employee. Since all parties concede that not just any Tom, Dick or Harry would be willing to assume this position, it is decided that Harold will receive one-third of the corporation's shares in return for entering into an employment contract with the corporation. Although this arrange-

ment may seem extremely fair under the circumstances, the California Corporations Code, as we've said, does not allow shares to be issued in return for future services, and Harold will have to contribute something else of value for his shares. Harold suggests that the corporation issue its shares to him in return for a long-term promissory note (he'll pay for them after he's survived a few tours). But, since shares cannot normally be issued in return for promissory notes without sufficient collateral to secure the deal, this idea is discarded, and Harold decides to pay (or borrow) enough cash to purchase his shares outright.

FUTURE WAYS TO RAISE ADDITIONAL CAPITAL

The corporate structure is designed to accommodate various capital interests. For example, you can issue common, voting shares to the initial owner-employees, set up a special nonvoting class of shares to distribute to key employees as an incentive to remain loyal to the business, and issue yet another preferred class of stock (one that gives investors a preference if dividends are declared or when the corporation is sold) to venture capitalists willing to help fund future expansion of your corporation.

And, increasingly, owners of a small corporation can set their sights someday on making a public offering of shares. Even if your corporation never grows large enough to interest a conventional stock underwriting company in selling your shares as part of a large public offering, you may be able to market your shares to your customers or to individual investors by placing your company's small offering prospectus on the Internet—something that has now been approved by the SEC (the federal Securities and Exchange Commission). This type of limited public offering is known as a "direct public offering" and is considerably more manageable and less expensive than the traditional underwritten public offering process usually only available to high-growth or high-tech startups.

Please see a lawyer if you are interested in setting up different classes of stock or offering stock through a direct public offering. The forms in this book cannot be used to use these sophisticated methods, which are often set up after forming a corporation.

But, of course, raising equity capital by selling stock is not the only way that corporations shine. Incorporated businesses also have an easier time than partnerships and LLCs in obtaining loans from banks and other capital investment firms (assuming a corporation's business plan or balance sheet and cash flow statements look good). That's partially due to the increased structural formality of the corporation (discussed in Section A4 above). In addition, loans can be made part of a package where the bank or investment company obtains special rights to choose one or more board members, or has special voting prerogatives in matters of corporate governance or finance. For example, a lender may require veto power over expenditures exceeding a specified amount. The range of capital arrangements possible, even for a small corporation, is limitless, giving the corporation its well-known knack for attracting outside investment.

EMPLOYEES OFTEN PREFER TO WORK FOR CORPORATIONS

Also, don't forget that key employees are more likely to work for a business that offers them a chance to profit (if future growth is strong) through the issuance of stock options and stock bonuses—financial incentives that only the corporate form can provide.

CORPORATIONS IN ACTION—SAL'S MIMEO CENTER

Here is another example that shows how several of the corporate characteristics discussed above can come in handy to accommodate the financial interests of different owners, while allowing a business to adapt to changing circumstances:

Sal Sr. and his son, Sal Jr., co-own and run Sal's Mimeo and Copy Center, a family business run for over 30 years as a partnership with a minimum of legal paperwork (in fact, before Sal Jr. joined the partnership firm, Sal Sr. ran the business as a sole proprietorship). Sal Sr. is retiring, letting Sal Jr., a business school grad, take over operational control.

Sal Jr. plans to expand the business by bringing in two business school friends, Ellen and Wilbur, as investors. Sal Jr. will contribute the business and its assets (including a long-term commercial lease to its storefront location and goodwill), to the new operation, while continuing to work as full-time manager of the business. The new capital will be used to expand into desktop publishing aimed at both the small business and the student markets.

Ellen and Wilbur will invest cash in two ways: each will pay cash in return for ownership interests, and each will also lend money to the business in exchange for promissory notes, which will be repaid by the firm. Interest only will be paid by the business on the notes over a five-year period, with repayment of the principal amount at the end of the loan term. Ellen and Wilbur hope that in five to seven years they can sell their interests back to Sal Jr. at a greatly increased book value price, or to another company wishing to buy into Sal's business. In the meantime, they are content to look to the interest payments on their notes as an adequate return on their investment in the business.

Sal Jr., seeing that a change in business structure is needed to give Ellen and Wilbur a stake in the business, decides to incorporate. The investors like the corporate form, since it limits their personal liability for its debts and other liabilities. Incorporating also should give the business a lift in its lending status at the local bank, which likes the fact that Sal Jr. is formalizing and expanding his business operations. Sal Jr. also realizes that forming a corporation will have tax advantages, since it is one good way to split business income between the business entity, the investors and himself. Specifically, the corporate form allows Sal to leave profits in the business, part of which will be used to pay back and retire Ellen's and Wilbur's promissory notes. In addition, the corporation will get to deduct Sal's salary and fringe benefits (as well as those of his employees) as well as the interest paid on the investors' notes. In short, the corporate form, with its built-in limited liability legal status, income- and tax-splitting capability, and stock ownership structure, suits Sal's new business needs to a T.

B. Corporate Tax Treatment

The corporate person is a separate taxpayer, with its own income tax rates and tax returns, different from the tax rates and tax returns of its owners. This separate layer of taxation allows corporate profits to be kept in the business and taxed at initial corporate tax rates that are generally lower than those of the corporation's owners. Business income-splitting between the corporation and its owners—attributing some income as corporate profit and paying out other income as salaries and bonuses—can result in an overall tax savings for the owners (compared to the pass-through taxation of all business profits to the owners, which is the standard tax treatment of sole proprietorships, partnerships and LLCs, where all income is taxed to the owners on their personal returns).

Example: *Jeff and Sally own and work for their own two-person corporation, Hair Looms, Inc., a mail-order wig supply business that is starting to enjoy popularity with overseas purchasers. To keep pace with the surge in orders, they need to expand by reinvesting a portion of their profits back in the business. Since Hair Looms is incorporated, only the portion of the profits paid to Jeff and Sally* *as salary is reported and taxed to them on their individual tax returns—let's assume, at the highest individual tax rate of 39.6 %. In contrast, the first $50,000 in profits left in the business for expansion is reported on Hair Looms' corporate income tax return, and is taxed at the lowest corporate tax rate of only 15%, and the next $25,000 at 25%. Above $75,000, corporate income is taxed at 34% and possibly higher, in highly profitable corporations. This allows Jeff and Sally to allot a portion of their profits for reinvestment, while paying a low corporate tax on those profits.*

1. How Small Corporations Avoid Double Taxation of Corporate Profits

What about the old bugaboo of corporate double taxation? Most people have heard that corporate income is taxed twice: once at the corporate level and again a second time when earnings are paid out to shareholders in the form of dividends. In practice, however, double taxation seldom occurs in the context of the small business corporation. The reason is simple. Employee-owners don't choose to pay themselves dividends. Instead, they pay themselves salaries and bonuses, in return for services rendered to their corporation. The salaries and bonuses are deducted from the profits of the corporate business as ordinary and necessary business expenses. The result is that profits paid out as salary and other forms of employee compensation to the owners of a small corporation are taxed only once, at the owner's individual tax rates. In other words, as long as you work for your corporation, even in a part-time or consulting capacity, you can pay out business profits to yourself as reasonable compensation instead of taking dividends, avoiding having your corporation pay taxes on these profits.

2. Smaller Corporations Can Elect S Corporation Tax Treatment

Most smaller corporations can change their built-in dual income tax treatment to the type of pass-through

taxation of business profits that normally applies to partnerships and LLCs. A corporation achieves this by making an S corporation tax election with the IRS (by filing IRS Form 2553). To qualify for S corporation tax treatment, the corporation must have 75 or fewer shareholders who are U.S. citizens or residents, and must meet other technical requirements. Once an S corporation election is made with the IRS, a California S corporation tax election can be made with the California Franchise Tax Board, which results in the corporation paying a 1.5% (instead of a 8.84%) state franchise tax on net corporate income earned in California.

A corporation that elects S corporation tax status has its profits, losses, credits and deductions passed through to its shareholders, who report these items on their individual tax returns. In effect, the S corporation election allows the corporation to side-step corporate taxes on business profits, passing the profits and the taxes that go with them along to the shareholders. Each S corporation shareholder is allocated a portion of profits and losses of the corporation according to her percentage of stock ownership in the corporation (a 50% shareholder reports and pays individual income taxes on 50% of the corporation's annual profits). Note that corporate profits are allocated annually to the shareholders whether the profits are actually paid to them or kept in the corporation.

Example: Fred's Furniture and Appliance was incorporated during a period of fast business growth at a time when Fred brought in two relatives as investors and moved his business to a larger storefront in an upscale neighborhood (with a renovated business name of "Frederick's Interiors, Inc."). He found the corporate form handy to limit his and the investors' personal liability and to accommodate his investors by issuing them shares in his business. With the business growing fast, the investors wanted to see some return of profits. To avoid paying dividends and the resulting double taxation, Fred elects S corporation tax treatment. Now, net profits of the business pass through to the S shareholders directly, and are taxed on their individual income tax returns. This meets the investors' needs, and avoids the double tax that would have been paid if profits were distributed to the investors as dividends. This also helps Fred, since he can keep his corporate salary low and still get other money out of his corporation (as a shareholder, he is allocated a percentage of the S corporation's profits too). Further, S corporation profits allocated to shareholders, unlike salaries, are not subject to self-employment taxes, so Fred ends up with more after-tax money in his pocket.

LLCS AND PARTNERSHIPS HAVE TECHNICAL TAX ADVANTAGES OVER S CORPORATIONS

If you are reading between the lines, you may have noticed that S corporations look and behave taxwise very much like LLCs and limited partnerships—all provide limited liability protection to investors and result in pass-through taxation of business profits. But LLCs and partnerships have some technical tax advantages over S corporations. For one, LLC owners and partners can split profits disproportionately to ownership interests in the business (these are called "special allocations" of profits and losses under the tax code); S corporation shareholders can't. Also, the amount of losses that may be passed through to S corporation shareholders is limited to the total of each shareholder's "basis" in his stock (the amount he paid for his stock plus and minus adjustments during the life of the corporation) plus amounts loaned personally by each shareholder to the corporation. Losses allocated to a shareholder that exceed these limits must be carried forward and deducted in future tax years if the shareholder then qualifies to deduct the excess losses. In contrast, LLC owners and partners may be able to personally deduct more business losses on their tax returns in a given year than S corporation shareholders. The reason is that an LLC member or a partner gets to count her pro-rata share of all money borrowed by the business, not just loans personally made by the member or partner, in computing how much of any loss allocated to her by the business she can deduct in a given year on her individual income tax return. Your tax advisor can fill you in on these details if you want more information.

---

3. Owners Who Work in the Business Are Treated as Employees

A key tax characteristic of the corporate structure is that business owners who also work in the business become employees. This means that you, in your role as an employee, become eligible for tax-deductible corporate fringe benefits, some of which you would not qualify for as a sole proprietor, partner or LLC member.

Example: Henry incorporates his California sole proprietorship, "Big Sur Shoes, Inc." He now works as a full-time corporate employee, and is entitled to unique tax-deductible corporate perks, such as reimbursement for medical expenses, 100% deductibility of health insurance premiums (health insurance premiums are currently only partially tax-deductible by unincorporated business owners) and group-term life insurance paid for by his business. If he gave himself these perks in his unincorporated business, his business could deduct them as ordinary and necessary business expenses, but he would have to report them as income and pay income taxes on them.

C. Corporate Securities Laws

Shares of stock of a corporation (one form of "securities") must be offered and sold in compliance with federal and state securities laws, which are directed at protecting prospective purchasers of shares by requiring full disclosure of information about the shares and making sure the transaction is fair. For large public offerings, the state and federal laws require you to register your stock issuance with the California Department of Corporations and the federal Securities and Exchange Commission—a task that can be expensive and time consuming. Luckily, many small corporations can avoid this for their initial issuance of shares, by using state and federal securities law exemptions that allow you to issue the initial shares of your corporation to your shareholders with a minimum of red tape and expense. In this section, we'll describe the exemptions and what your corporation and your shareholders need to do to qualify for them.

To be able to use this book (and the stock issuance process described in Chapter 6) to issue shares, you must meet the requirements of the state and federal exemptions discussed below. If you find that you do not so qualify after reading the following discussions, or if you have any questions or doubts, please consult a lawyer to determine whether you must use another state and/or federal exemption to issue your initial shares or whether you'll be required to register your stock issuance with the California Department of Corporations and the federal Securities and Exchange Commission. Fortunately, most incorporators using this book to form a small corporation will issue shares privately, only to the founders of the corporation and, perhaps, to immediate family members, and so should qualify for the state and federal exemptions we cover here.

DISCLOSE ALL MATERIAL FACTS SURROUNDING THE ISSUANCE OF YOUR SHARES

Section 25401 of the California Corporations Code states: "It is unlawful for any person to offer or sell a security in this state or buy or offer to buy a security in this state by means of any written or oral communication which includes an untrue statement of a material fact or omits to state a material fact necessary in order to make the statements made, in light of the circumstances under which they were made, not misleading." The federal Securities Act contains similar anti-fraud provisions. Both state and federal law impose penalties and personal liability if the disclosure requirements of the securities laws are violated. So, make sure you are completely honest in your dealings with potential shareholders, and that you disclose all material facts concerning your incorporation and share issuance to potential stock purchasers.

---

1. The California "Limited Offering" Stock Exemption

Section 25102(f) of the California Corporations Code contains an exemption for the offer and sale of securities called the "limited offering exemption" that you can rely on to issue your initial shares. The regulations that have been promulgated in order to clarify the meaning of this statutory exemption statute are contained in Title 10 of the California Code of Regulations, Sections 260.102.2 through 260.102.14.

The limited offering exemption is for *private* issuances of shares, and is generally available if you will be issuing shares privately, *without advertisements or public solicitation, to people who can protect their own financial interests.* Let's look at the basic requirements your stock issuance and stock purchasers must meet:

- All purchasers of shares issued under the limited offering exemption are required to represent that they are purchasing their shares for their own investment and not with an intent toward resale (such as buying and selling shares on a national stock exchange). This investment representation must be made in writing by each prospective shareholder. This investment representation is included in the shareholder representation letter included with this book—we show you how to fill in the letter in Chapter 6, Section A.

- The offer or sale of shares must not be accompanied by the publication of any advertisement. The California Corporations Code defines "advertisement" to mean any written or printed communication or any communication by means of recorded telephone messages or spoken on radio, television, or similar communication media, that are published in connection with the offer or sale of a security. "Publish" means to issue or circulate publicly by newspaper, mail, radio or television, or otherwise to disseminate to the public. Although these terms cover a lot of ground, generally, you may circulate information regarding the stock, the corporation and the transaction (such as offering circulars and disclosure documents) to a select group of prospective purchasers, so long as these materials are not disseminated to the public. To stay within the rules, the disclosure of material about your stock issuance should be limited to persons reasonably believed to be interested in purchasing the shares and to "suitable" prospective purchasers (see below). In other words, use common sense in communicating the fact that you are setting up a corporation and will be issuing your initial shares, keeping these types of discussions with potential investors on a private level and not disclosing the availability of your shares in any public way.

- A form issued by the state called Notice of Transaction under Section 25102(f) must be filed with the Department of Corporations within 15 calendar days after the first sale of a stock in California. This notice form is included with this book—we show you how to fill it out and file it in Chapter 6, Section B.

- Your prospective purchasers must be "suitable"— that is, they must fit within one or more categories defined under the limited offering exemption statute and regulations. As you'll see, the basic purpose of these categories is to ensure that each of your shareholders is able to protect herself when purchasing shares in your corporation. Here is a list of the categories of suitable purchasers most likely to apply to the initial stock issuance of smaller corporations (as you'll see, all of your shareholders will probably fit into the first three or four categories, so you won't need to be concerned with the later, more complicated categories involving more professional investors).

Promoters of the Corporation. These are people who take the initiative in founding and organizing the business or enterprise of the corporation (including the Incorporator—the person who signs and files the Articles of Incorporation). Readers of this book who form their own corporation should be considered the promoters of their corporation.

Directors and Officers of the Corporation. Many smaller corporations issue initial shares only to the directors and officers of the newly formed corporation. In this case, all initial shareholders are suitable under the limited offering exemption. Also, people who function more or less as officers but who have different titles (executives and managerial or supervisory employees) are suitable shareholders.

Relatives of Another Suitable Shareholder. Spouses, relatives or relatives of the spouses (in-laws) of another suitable shareholder who have the same principal residence as this other shareholder are, themselves, considered suitable as shareholders under the California limited offering exemption. The term "relative" means a person who is related by blood, marriage or adoption.

Individuals With a Pre-existing Personal or Business Relationship With the Corporation or Any of its Officers, Directors or Promoters. To fit into this category, a person must know one of the above people connected to the corporation well enough "to be aware of the character, business acumen and general business and financial circumstances of the person." The relationship of employer-employee does not automatically meet this test (for example, if you issue shares to someone who is already an employee of the business, you can't assume that this person meets this relationship requirement). *Note that you cannot issue shares to more than 35 persons who fit within this category.*

Investors With Professional Advisors. These are persons who, by reason of the business or financial experience of their professional advisor, can be assumed to have the capacity to protect their interests in connection with the purchase of stock. A professional advisor is defined as an attorney, a certified accountant or "a person who, as a regular part of such person's business, is customarily relied upon by others for investment recommendations or decisions, and who is customarily compensated for such services." Besides lawyers and CPAs, here are some other examples of professional advisors: persons licensed or registered as broker-dealers and agents, investment advisers and banks and savings and loan associations. Any professional advisor must be unaffiliated with, and must not be compensated by, the corporation itself. If a shareholder relies upon a professional advisor to qualify as a suitable shareholder under this category, she must designate the advisor in writing. The shareholder representation letter included with this book allows a shareholder to designate a professional advisor—we show you how to fill in this letter in Chapter 6, Section A. *Note that you cannot issue shares to more than 35 persons who fit within this category.*

Sophisticated Investors. These are individuals who, because of their business or financial experience, can be assumed to have the capacity to protect their interests in connection with the stock issuance transaction. *Note that you cannot issue shares to more than 35 persons who fit within this category.*

Major Investors. These are persons who purchase $150,000 or more of the corporation's shares, who either have the capacity (or professional advisors)

to protect their interests in connection with the stock purchase, or whose investments do not exceed 10% of their net worth (the net worth of the investor's spouse can be included in this computation). (Note there is no limit to the number of major investors you can issue shares to.)

Accredited (Wealthy) Investors. These are: 1) persons whose individual net worth, or joint net worth with their spouse, exceeds $1,000,000 at the time of the purchase of stock, or 2) persons who have had an individual income in excess of $200,000 in each of the two most recent years (or joint income with their spouse in excess of $300,000 in each of those years), and who have a reasonable expectation of reaching the same income level in the current year. (Note there is no limit to the number of accredited investors you can issue shares to.)

⚠️ SALES OF STOCK TO 35 OR FEWER SHAREHOLDERS

Notice that a few of the categories of suitable shareholders under the limited offering exemption are limited to 35 or fewer shareholders. We need to amplify this point as follows: You cannot issue shares under the limited offering exemption to more than a *total* of 35 persons who fit within any suitability category that is restricted to 35 of fewer shares. In other words, this restriction is cumulative. For example, if you issue shares to 30 persons who have a pre-existing business relationship with the directors of the corporation, you cannot issue shares to more than five other persons who are either sophisticated investors or merely have professional advisors (each of these latter two categories is also restricted to 35 or fewer persons). This added wrinkle to the rules should not be a problem for two reasons: 1) most smaller corporations will issue shares to a total of 35 or fewer persons, and 2) spouses who are issued shares under the limited offering exemption are counted as one person, not two, in applying this 35-or-fewer rule.

USING THE RULES OF THE CALIFORNIA LIMITED OFFERING EXEMPTION

It should be easy to determine if your initial stock issuance will meet most of the rules listed above of the California limited exemption. The only difficult part involves making sure each of your shareholders fits within a suitable shareholder category. Here is what we recommend in making this assessment:

- If you will only issue shares to directors, officers and/or their relatives (as defined by the rules), you should feel safe in utilizing this exemption.
- If you need to qualify an investor under one of the other categories, such as an investor with a pre-existing relationship to corporate directors or officers, or a sophisticated, major or accredited investor, check your conclusion with a lawyer. These other categories are subjective legal standards and financial tests that require further analysis.
- For more information, including examples of how a small corporation can utilize the limited offering exemption, see the expanded treatment of this exemption in *How to Form Your Own California Corporation,* by Anthony Mancuso (Nolo Press).

OTHER CALIFORNIA STOCK OFFERING EXEMPTIONS

If you cannot meet the requirements of the California limited offering exemption to issue the initial shares of your corporation, you should discuss the availability of other California stock offering procedures with a lawyer, including the following:

- **The California "Small Offering Exemption."** This is a private stock offering available under Section 25102(h) of the California Corporations Code to a corporation that will be issuing stock to 35 or fewer shareholders for cash. A corporation that relies on this exemption must have a lawyer sign an "Opinion of Counsel" statement on a notice form that is filed with the Department of Corporations, stating that in the lawyer's opinion, the stock offering and issuance meets the requirements of the small offering exemption.
- **The California "Limited Public Offering."** Section 25102(n) of the Corporations Code allows corporations to make a general announcement of the sale of shares to the public, provided certain conditions related to the information in the announcement and its dissemination to the public are met. Two notice forms must be filed to rely on this exemption; one of which requires a filing fee of $600. Generally, the purchasers of shares must:
- qualify as suitable shareholders under the various categories of the California limited offering exemption (the main exemption discussed in the text above) or
- have a net worth of $250,000 or more and gross annual income of $100,000 or greater. Those in this latter group are limited to making an investment of no more than 10% or their net worth and must be given specific disclosure material at least five business days before the sale of shares.
- **Simplified Permit Procedure for Small Public Offering.** California Corporations Code Section 25113(b)(2) allows a corporation to raise up to $1 million in a small public offering by filing a relatively simple question-and-answer form, Form U-7, commonly referred to as a Small Corporate Offering Registration (or SCOR) form with the California Department of Corporations. Since this is not an exemption, but a simplified permit procedure, a fee of $2,500 is charged, plus up to $1,000 more, based upon the Department's average cost of processing the form for all SCOR applicants. Use of Form U-7 is being recognized in a number of other states, and may soon be the best way to obtain moderate amounts of public equity capital from investors under state securities registration laws. Note: The minimum stock price under this procedure is $5, proceeds from the sale of shares must be used in the business and the corporation must have only one class of shares of voting common stock outstanding after the SCOR issuance.

2. The Federal "Private Offering" Exemption

Your initial stock issuance must also comply with the federal Securities Act. You must register your initial offering of stock with the federal Securities and Exchange Commission (SEC) unless you fall under a specific exemption from registration. Traditionally, most small, closely held corporations wishing to privately issue their initial shares to a limited number of people have been able to rely on the federal "private offering" exemption (also called the federal "nonpublic offering" exemption). As discussed below, we assume that readers using this book who will be eligible for the California limited offering exemption (the main exemption we discussed in the section just above) will also qualify for this federal exemption since, as you'll see, the basic requirements of the two exemptions are similar. Let's look at the general requirements of this federal exemption.

The Federal Securities Act, in Section 4(2), simply says that the federal private offering exemption is available for stock transaction where a public offering is not involved. To clarify this law, the courts have discussed the basic elements that should be present when relying on this exemption. (After reading the rules below, if you're not sure whether you'll qualify for this exemption and are interested in the details, a leading case is *SEC v. Ralston Purina Co.,* 346 U.S. 119 (1953).)

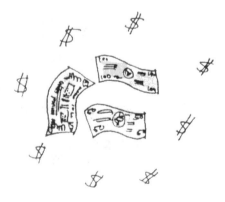

- The prospective purchasers (persons to whom shares are offered) must be able to fend for themselves due to their previous financial or business experience, their relationship to the issuer (the corporation, its directors, officers), and/or their significant personal net worth;
- The transaction must truly be a nonpublic offering involving no general advertising or solicitation;
- The shares must be purchased by the shareholders for their own investment purposes and not with the intent to resell them;
- The prospective purchasers must be limited in number;
- The prospective purchasers must have access to or be given information relevant to the stock transaction in order to evaluate the pros and cons of the investment.

Again, if your private offering meets the requirements of the California limited offering exemption, you should feel safe in most cases treating your issuance as a private offering under the federal rules. But if you have any doubts or questions, ask a lawyer. If you wish to feel safer, the lawyer can help you prepare and file a notice form under Regulation D (see the sidebar, "Federal Regulation D Exemption Rules and Procedures") to secure a federal limited offering exemption.

STOCK CERTIFICATE LEGENDS

The stock certificates included with this book contain a legend stating that the shares have been purchased for investment purposes and not for resale, that they have not been registered under state and federal securities laws and that they cannot be transferred without being registered or qualifying for an exemption from registration. This legend should help establish that your initial stock issuance is a private offering under the federal guidelines.

FEDERAL REGULATION D EXEMPTION RULES AND PROCEDURES

Federal Regulation D contains a series of federal stock offering and issuance exemption rules. Small corporations often decide to use Regulation D to officially notify the Securities and Exchange Commission that they qualify for an exemption under one of the Regulation D rules (by filing Form D, Notice of Sales of Securities, with the SEC). Utilizing Regulation D gives incorporators an extra measure of certainty that their stock issuance complies with the federal Securities Act. Rule 506, below, is the most obvious exemption rule to rely on and most closely resembles the California limited offering exemption. Here is a very brief look at these Regulation D exemption rules:

- Rule 504 exempts limited offerings up to $1 million from federal registration. No general advertising is permitted, this rule does not limit the number of purchasers, and no more than $500,000 of the stock can be sold without registering the sale with the *state*.
- Rule 505 exempts limited offerings up to $5 million. No general advertising is permitted, generally no more than 35 nonaccredited investors are allowed and specific information must be disclosed if any nonaccredited investors are included in the offering.
- Rule 506 does not contain a specific limit on the total dollar amount of the stock issuance. Under Rule 506, shares cannot be offered or sold by any form of general solicitation or advertising, and there can be no more than 35 purchasers of shares. However, certain purchasers of shares are not counted toward this 35-shareholder limit, including:
- certain "accredited investors," including directors and executive officers of the corporation, and individuals with a net worth of more than $1 million or with two years' prior individual income in excess of $200,000 (or joint income with a spouse in excess of $300,000).
- the spouses, relatives and relatives of spouses of another suitable purchaser if they share the same principal residence as the other purchaser.

The corporation must reasonably believe that each purchaser who is not an accredited investor has such knowledge and experience in financial matters that he is capable of evaluating the merits and risks of the prospective investment. Like the California limited offering exemption (the main exemption discussed in Section 1 above), this rule allows a purchaser to rely on the experience of a professional advisor (called a "purchaser representative"), who must be designated in writing. Perhaps the most significant procedural differences between the California limited offering exemption and Rule 506 is that federal law requires a corporation to furnish specific types of information (including financial statements, written disclosure of resale restrictions) to nonaccredited investors within a reasonable time prior to sale of the shares (to be safe, this information should be disclosed to accredited investors as well). Also, purchasers must be given the opportunity to ask questions and receive answers concerning the terms and conditions of the offering and to obtain any additional information that is necessary to verify the accuracy of information already furnished to the purchaser.

D. Downsides of Incorporating

Just about everything, including the advantages of incorporating, comes at a price. And, of course, the answer to the question "How much does it cost?" is an important factor to weigh when considering whether to incorporate your business. For starters, a corporation, unlike a sole proprietorship or general partnership, requires the filing of formation papers—Articles of Incorporation—with the California Secretary of State. The filing cost is $900 ($100 filing fee plus $800 minimum first-year franchise tax payment; some corporations qualify for a reduced initial tax payment of $600, which lowers the total filing fee to $700—see

Chapter 3), and you must pay an annual minimum tax of $800 to the Franchise Tax Board each year (some corporations qualify for a reduced second-year minimum tax of $500).

Ongoing paperwork is generally not burdensome, but, unlike a sole proprietorship, attention must be paid to holding and documenting annual meetings of shareholders and directors and keeping minutes of important corporate meetings. Creating this paper trail is a good way to show the IRS, in case of an audit, or the courts, in case of a lawsuit that tries to hold shareholders personally liable, that you have respected the corporate form and are entitled to claim (hide behind) its insulating layer of limited personal liability.

HELP WITH ONGOING CORPORATE FORMALITIES

One way to take care of ongoing corporate paperwork at minimal expense is to use *The Corporate Minutes Book: A Legal Guide to Taking Care of Corporate Business,* by Anthony Mancuso (Nolo Press). This book shows you how to prepare standard minutes of annual and special director and shareholder meetings for an existing corporation. It also contains resolutions to approve the various legal, tax, financial and business transactions that commonly occur during the life of a small corporation. All forms and resolutions are provided as tear-outs and forms on disk.

The other main disadvantage of incorporating has traditionally been the $1,000 to $2,000 (sometimes more) you could expect to pay an attorney for creating the initial paperwork. This book, together with a little effort on your part, should significantly reduce, if not eliminate, this cost.

E. Does It Make Sense to Incorporate Out of State?

Before concluding this introductory material, we want to highlight an issue that crops up during the startup phase of many small corporations—whether to incorporate in California or out-of-state.

You have no doubt have heard about the possibility of incorporating in Delaware, Nevada, or another state where initial and ongoing fees are lower and regulations may be less restrictive than in California. Does this make sense? For large, publicly held corporations looking for the most lenient statutes and courts to help them fend off corporate raiders, perhaps yes. But for a small, privately held corporation pursuing an active California business, our answer is no—it is usually a very poor idea to incorporate out-of-state. The big reason is that, if you incorporate out of state, you would have to qualify to do business in California anyway, and this process takes about as much time, and costs as much money as filing incorporation papers in California in the first place. You'd also need to appoint a corporate agent to receive official corporate notices in the state where you incorporate—another expensive pain in the neck.

It is also important to realize that incorporating in another state with a lower corporate income tax isn't likely to save you any money. That's because if your business makes money from operations in California, even if it is incorporated in another state, you still must pay California taxes on this income.

Example: Best Greeting Card, Inc., plans to open a Jenner, California, facility to design and market holiday greeting cards throughout the country. If it incorporates in Delaware, it must qualify to do business in California (and pay a fee), and pay California corporate income tax on income from its California operations. It also must hire a registered agent to act on its behalf in Delaware. It decides to incorporate in California instead.

So, unless you plan to open up a business with offices and operations in more than one state and, therefore, have a real reason to compare corporate domiciles, you should stay where you are, and incorporate in your home state—California. ∎

Choose a Corporate Name

With this chapter, we begin explaining the steps necessary to form your own California business corporation. The first step is choosing a name for your corporation—also called your corporate name. Besides picking a name for your business that you like, this involves making sure the name you want to use meets the corporate name requirements of the California Secretary of State, and is available for your use when you file Articles of Incorporation (which is also when you'll file your corporate name). We also show you how to take reasonable measures to make sure no other business will take umbrage at your choice of a corporate name, and where to go to protect your name against use by others.

A. Choose a Likable Corporate Name

The first step in choosing a corporate name is finding one that you like. Your corporate name is important, because it will identify the "goodwill" of your business. We don't mean this in any strict legal or accounting sense, but simply that the people you do business with, including your customers, clients, other merchants, vendors, independent contractors, lenders and the business community in general will identify your business primarily by your name. For this reason, as well as a number of practical reasons, such as not wanting to print new stationery, change Yellow Pages or advertising copy or create new logos or purchase new signs, you will want to pick a name that you will be happy with for a long time. So pay particular attention to your choice of a corporate name—as a practical matter, it's likely to become one of your most important assets. But don't get your heart set on a name until you make sure it's available for use—we tell you how to do this in the rest of this chapter.

DO YOUR OWN MARKET RESEARCH

Before you finally commit to a name, get some feedback from customers, suppliers and others in your support network. Other pairs of ears may come up with a downside or a suggestion for improvement you haven't thought of.

B. Comply With the Secretary of State's Name Formalities

Generally, a California business corporation is not required to use a "corporate designator" in its corporate name, such as "Corporation," "Incorporated" or "Limited," or an abbreviation of one of these words ("Corp.," "Inc." or "Ltd."). But many incorporators (the corporation's founders) will wish to use one of these designators precisely because they want others to know that their business is incorporated. In fact, if your business is already in operation as a sole proprietorship or partnership, it is likely that you will wish simply to adopt the name of your unincorporated business as your corporate name, adding a corporate designator to the end.

Example: *The partners of Best Furniture decide to incorporate their store (which they were running as a partnership up until now) under the name, Best Furniture, Inc.*

There is one large exception to this general rule, however. If your corporate name includes the name of a person, it must have a corporate designator, such as "Incorporated," "Inc.," "Corporation," "Corp.," "Limited," or "Ltd." For example, "Biff Baxter" would be an

invalid corporate name, but "Biff Baxter, Inc.," would be acceptable. We discuss another point related to individual corporate names in the sidebar titled "Using Your Individual Name in Your Corporate Name," in Section C, below.

Lastly, a California corporation cannot use certain words in its name that are reserved for special types of corporations in California. Among these restricted words are the following:

Bank	Reserve
Cooperative	Trust
Federal	Trustee
National	United States

C. Make Sure Another Company Doesn't Have Legal Rights to Your Proposed Name

Although you must submit your name to the Secretary of State for approval (as we explain in Section D below), just because the Secretary of State approves your corporate name doesn't necessarily mean that you have the legal right to use this name. The Secretary of State's office simply checks its corporate name files to make sure your name doesn't conflict with that of another corporation already on file with the Secretary of State. The Secretary of State does not check proposed corporate names to see if they conflict with the names of *unincorporated* businesses in existence in California (including sole proprietorships, partnerships and LLCs), nor does it check names that businesses have registered as trademarks or service marks (see "What is a Trademark or Service Mark?" below) with the California Secretary of State or U.S. Patent and Trademark Office. In short, another incorporated or unincorporated business could be using your proposed name to identify its own business, goods or services, but it wouldn't show up during the Secretary of State's name availability check.

WHAT IS A TRADEMARK OR SERVICE MARK?

A **trademark** (sometimes called simply a **"mark"**) is any word or phrase used to market a product or service. Technically, a mark used to market a service is called a **"service mark,"** though the term "trademark" is commonly used for both types of marks. For instance, "Harley Davidson" is a trademark used by the Harley Davidson company to market motorcycles, and "Smog Pros" is a service mark used by Arco to market its smog-check service centers.

To fill in these gaps, you'll have to do some investigation of your own to see if another incorporated or unincorporated business has the legal right to use your proposed corporate name. Who has the legal right to a name or trademark? The basic rule is that the ultimate right to use a particular business name hinges on who was first in time to actually use the name in connection with a particular trade, business, service or product. As a result, when you're choosing your corporate name, you've got to check each possible name to see if someone else has dibs on it. Unfortunately, deciding whether another company has rights to a name can get a bit complicated. That's because, not only can you not use the exact name another company is already using, you can't use a name that is too similar to it.

How do you decide whether the name you have chosen as a corporate name is too similar to another name? Here's our recommendation: simply ask yourself whether an outsider, such as a customer or client of another business, might reasonably confuse your proposed name with a business name or trademark that already exists, and thereby deal with the wrong business. If you're honest, you can provide as good a guideline for yourself as any lawyer who specializes in this area of law.

In deciding whether a name is too similar to an existing business's name, the types of businesses and their geographical proximity are also important factors. For example, if you plan to operate the "Sears Massage School, Inc.," you probably won't have a problem at least as far as the well-known retail chain is concerned—obviously, you are in a different line of business than the well-known retail products chain. But, if your corporate name is "Sears Sales and Service, Inc.," watch out! The big retail chain will undoubtedly ask you to change your name to avoid confusion by the public and to thwart your ability to capitalize on their reputation and goodwill.

AVOID NATIONALLY KNOWN NAMES TO AVOID FUTURE CONFLICTS

Keep in mind that we live in an age where a huge number of service businesses—muffler shops, smog-check stations, eyeglass stores and house-cleaning services to cite just a few examples—are being purchased by large national franchise chains. Even if your corporate name does not now conflict with a nearby existing business, it may in a few years when a national chain or franchise with a similar name sets up shop in your area. So stay away from nationally known franchise or chain store names. Even if you think you have the right to use the name because you used it first in your area, these stores and their lawyers have a lot of time and money on their hands, and can make your life miserable until the issue is settled in or out of court.

THE INTERNET MAKES FINDING A SAFE NAME MORE DIFFICULT

In today's world of the Internet and mail-order catalog businesses, the idea of "local" isn't what it used to be. Even if you open a tiny book, card or video rental store in a small town, if you inadvertently choose the same name as an Internet store that your local customers can access, you may very well find yourself being accused of infringement of its trademark—even if the online store has its headquarters on a different continent.

USING YOUR INDIVIDUAL NAME IN YOUR CORPORATE NAME

The Secretary of State recognizes that individuals have special rights to the use of their names in connection with their businesses and, therefore, normally will allow two individuals with the same name to use them in their corporate title without raising the issue of similarity (two Baxter Paints, Inc.'s would probably be allowed by the Secretary of State). There is an exception to this rule, however, and to general principles of trademark law under state "dilution of trademark" statutes. Specifically, even if you use your own surname in your corporate name and even though your products, services and geographical area of operation and marketing are unrelated to those of another business, if your corporate name contains a word or phrase that is the same or similar to the name of another business's mark, it can seek to enjoin (stop) you from using your name on the theory that your use will dilute (weaken) the value of their mark. Without going into the technicalities here, our best advice, again, is to use common sense. If your proposed corporate name contains a word or phrase that is the same as a well-known mark, you may wish to add a word or phrase to your corporate name to make it clear that you are unaffiliated with the company that owns the mark (going back to the example above, the owners might decide to incorporate under the full name of the owner as "John P. Sears Massage School, Inc."). This issue will not arise for most incorporators. If it does, we suggest you check with a trademark lawyer.

To help you find names already in use by other businesses that are the same as or close to your proposed corporate name, it is wise to do a little informal checking on your own. Here are some self-help steps we recommend for researching your proposed name:

- First, to check unregistered trade names—the majority of names used by unincorporated businesses are not registered—use a common sense approach. Check major metropolitan phonebook listings, business and trade directories and other business listings, such as the Dun & Bradstreet

business listing. Larger public libraries have phone directories for many major cities within and outside of California. You can also use any search engine on the Internet, such as Yahoo!, AltaVista, InfoSeek or Excite, to quickly find out whether someone else on the Web is using a specific name.

- The California Secretary of State maintains separate databases of registered names for LLCs and limited partnerships (as we mentioned above, the Secretary of State's office will not check these databases when doing a corporate name check). These are good databases to check because you can do a search in person or by phone for free. Call 916-653-3794 to check on existing LLC names, and 916-653-3365 to check on existing partnership names.

- In addition, you can call the California Secretary of State's trademark/service mark registration section at 916-653-4984 to see if your proposed corporate name is already registered for use by another business. They will check up to two names over the phone at no charge.

- Check with the County Clerk in the county or counties in which you plan to do business to see if your name has already been registered by another person or business as a "fictitious business name" (a business name that's different from the legal name of the sole proprietor, partnership, LLC or corporation). Most County Clerks will require you to come in and check the files yourself—it takes just a few minutes to do this and it's free. Also, a new site on the Internet allows you to search fictitious business names registered in all counties in California at one time for $10 per name. Point your browser to http://www.merlindata.com and look for *California Statewide Fictitious Business Names Search* under online databases.

- Go to a public library or special business and government library in your area that carries the federal Trademark Register, a listing of federal trademark/service marks broken into categories of goods and services. This aspect of your search is extremely important. You can search the federal Trademark Register yourself for free by pointing your Internet browser to the U.S. Patent and Trademark Office's Website at http://www1.uspto.gov/tmdb/index.html .

We think the above name search sources are likely to reveal most sources of name conflict, and should give you a good basis for deciding whether your choice of a corporate name is a safe one. If you want to check further or don't want to do it all yourself, you can pay a private records-search company to check federal and state trademarks and service marks as well as local and statewide business listings. Alternatively, or in conjunction with your own efforts or search procedures, you can pay a trademark lawyer to oversee or undertake these searches for you. An attorney will take the responsibility of hiring a private search company and may provide a legal opinion on the relative legal safety of your use of your proposed corporate name. Normally, this opinion isn't necessary, but it can be a valuable strategy if a name search discovers several similar, but not identical, names.

D. Check With the Secretary of State to See If Your Proposed Corporate Name Is Available

As mentioned above, the Secretary of State maintains a list of names of existing California corporations; out-of-state corporations who have qualified to do business in California (or registered their name with the California Secretary of State); and corporate names that have been reserved for use (in advance of incorporation or qualification to do business in California). If your name is the same as or similar to any of these, it will be rejected. For practical purposes, this means that your proposed corporate name cannot share one or more distinguishing words with a name already on the Secretary of State's corporate name list.

Example: If you wish to set up a wholesale house for computer equipment under the name "Compusell, Inc.," and a corporation is already on file with the Secretary of

State under the name "Compusel, International, Inc.," your name will probably be rejected by the Secretary of State for being too similar to the existing listed name.

You can check the availability of up to three corporate names by sending a letter to the Secretary of State's office in Sacramento. We have provided a tear-out name availability request letter in the Appendix of this book that you can use for this purpose. Complete the letter as you follow the sample form with instructions below.

➡ **YOU MAY WANT TO RESERVE YOUR CORPORATE NAME**
Even if the Secretary indicates by return mail that a corporate name is available, someone else may take it before you file your Articles. To avoid this problem, you can check and reserve a name for a fee as explained in the next subsection. You do not have to send the availability request letter as explained in this section. Skip ahead to Section E to reserve and check your proposed corporate name.

✔ The parenthetical blanks, i.e., "(information)," indicate information that you must complete on the form.
✔ Each circled number on the form (e.g., ❶) refers to a special instruction that provides specific information to help you complete an item. The special instructions immediately follow the sample form.
✔ Fill in the tear-out form using a typewriter or printer with a black-ink ribbon.

As mentioned in the introduction to this book, this letter and all of the tear-out forms included at the back of this book are available for purchase and download from the Nolo Press Website. See the introduction for more information.

NAME AVAILABILITY REQUEST LETTER

(*type name and address of
an initial director here*)

Secretary of State
Corporate Filing and Services Division
1500 11th Street
Sacramento, California 95814

Secretary of State:
Please advise if any of the following names are presently available for corporate use:
1. *(insert up to three choices for a proposed corporate name)*
2. _____
3. _____

I enclose a stamped, self-addressed envelope for your reply.
Sincerely,

_____
(*type the initial director's name here*)

IF A NAME YOU REALLY LIKE IS UNAVAILABLE

If the use of a particular corporate name is crucial to you and you are told that it is unavailable since it is deceptively similar to an existing name already on file with the Secretary of State, there are a few things you can do:

- Submit a written request for a review of your name's acceptability to the legal counsel's office at the Secretary of State. You should realize that deciding the legal question of whether or not a name is similar enough to a name used by another business to cause confusion to the public involves looking at a number of criteria contained in a long line of court decisions, including the nature of the two businesses and their geographical proximity.

  If you do get into this sort of squabble, you will probably want to see a lawyer who is versed in the complexities of business name or trademark law, or do some additional reading on your own. *Trademark, Legal Care for Your Business and Product Name*, by Attorneys Kate McGrath and Stephen Elias (Nolo Press) explains the rules and criteria in more detail.

- Obtain the written consent of the other corporation already using a corporate name that's similar to your proposed name. Before you bother doing this, call the Secretary of State at 916-657-5448 and ask a name availability clerk if this written consent procedure will work for you. Even with the consent of the other corporation, the Secretary's office will not allow you to use a similar name if they feel the public is likely to be misled (if the names sound very similar, for example). If you get the go-ahead to use this procedure, ask the name availability clerk for the address of the other corporation and then send your written request to that address for an officer of the other corporation to sign, together with an explanatory letter—and/or a preliminary phone call—indicating that you'd like them to agree to your use of your similar name and why you think it will not cause customer confusion (for example, because you will be engaged in a different line of business in a different locale).

- Decide that it's simpler and less trouble all the way around to pick another name for your business. We normally recommend this third approach when searching for an available corporate name.

E. Reserve Your Corporate Name

For a fee, you can reserve a corporate name with the Secretary of State before filing your articles. We think it makes sense to do this rather than simply checking to see if your name is available as explained above. When you submit a name reservation letter by mail with the Sacramento office of the Secretary of State's office, they will check the availability of up to three names and reserve the first available name. That name will be reserved exclusively for your use for a period of 60 days. The fee to reserve a name by mail for 60 days is $10.

In person. You can also reserve a corporate name in person at any one of the offices of the Secretary of State (see below). The fee for reserving a name in person is $20. The clerk will ask for *two* $10 checks—one as an administrative fee, the other as the regular fee for reserving a name. If your proposed name is not available, the clerk will only return one $10 check to you. Here are the Secretary of State's local office addresses and phone numbers:

Fresno

2497 West Shaw, Suite 101
Fresno, CA 93711
209-243-2100

Los Angeles

300 South Spring Street, Room 12513
Los Angeles, CA 90013-1233
213-897-3062

Sacramento

1500 11th Street
Sacramento, CA 95814
916-653-6814

San Diego

1350 Front Street, Suite 2060
San Diego, CA 92101-3690
619-525-4113

San Francisco

235 Montgomery Street, Suite 725
San Francisco, CA 94104
415-439-6959

WHAT IF THE 60-DAY RESERVATION PERIOD EXPIRES?

If you cannot file your Articles within the 60-day reservation period, you can re-reserve the name by preparing a new reservation letter and paying another fee. Note that a second reservation letter must be received by the Secretary of State at least one day after the first reservation period expires (the law does not allow two consecutive reservations of corporate name—therefore the requests must be separated by at least one day), so you should time the mailing of your second reservation request accordingly.

Simply use the tear-out letter in the Appendix of this book as you follow the instructions and sample form below.

✔ The parenthetical blanks, i.e., " (information) ," indicate information that you must complete on the form.

✔ Each circled number on the form (e.g., ❶) refers to a special instruction that provides specific information to help you complete an item. The special instructions immediately follow the sample form.

✔ Fill in the tear-out form using a typewriter or printer with a black-ink ribbon.

```
              REQUEST FOR RESERVATION OF CORPORATE NAME

(type name and address of an initial director here)


Secretary of State
Corporate Filing and Services Division
1500 11th Street
Sacramento, CA 95814


Secretary of State:
Please reserve the first available corporate name from the list below for my
use. My proposed corporate names, listed in order of preference, are as fol-
lows:
1. (insert up to three choices for a proposed
    corporate name, in order of preference)
2. _____
3. _____
I enclose a check or money order for the required reservation fee, payable to
the "Secretary of State."
Sincerely,

_____
(type the initial director's name here)
```

 AN INITIAL CORPORATE DIRECTOR SHOULD SIGN THE RESERVATION REQUEST LETTER

Make sure one of the people who will sign your Articles of Incorporation (one of your initial directors—see Chapter 3, Section A) prepares and signs your reservation request letter, since your corporate name will be reserved for use by the individual who signs this letter.

F. Protect Your Name

Once you have reserved a corporate name and filed your Articles of Incorporation, you may wish to take additional steps to protect your name. For example,

you may wish to register your corporate name with your local County Clerk as a fictitious business name (if you plan to do business under a name other than your corporate name). This provides another form of constructive notice to other businesses that your name is not available for their use.

If your name will be used to identify products that you sell, or services that you provide, you may wish to register it as a trademark or service mark with the California Secretary of State and the U.S. Patent and Trademark Office (registration in other states where you do business may also be appropriate). The trademark/service mark application procedures are relatively simple and reasonably inexpensive, and are fully explained in *Trademark, Legal Care for Your Business and Product Name*, by Attorneys Kate McGrath and Stephen Elias (Nolo Press). ■

File Articles of Incorporation

The next step in organizing your corporation is preparing and filing Articles of Incorporation with the California Secretary of State. Your corporation's legal life begins on the effective date of the filing of your Articles—normally, this is within one or two business days of the date your Articles are received by the Secretary of State's office (or the date you file your Articles over-the-counter at one of the Secretary of State's offices).

A. Prepare Articles of Incorporation

Let's get right to the form. Fill in the tear-out Articles in the Appendix as you follow the sample form and special instructions below. The information required to complete this form is remarkably basic and easy to provide.

✔ The parenthetical blanks, i.e., " *(information)* ," indicate information that you must complete on the form.

✔ Each circled number on the form (e.g., ❶) refers to a special instruction that provides specific information to help you complete an item. The special instructions immediately follow the sample form.

✔ Fill in the tear-out form using a typewriter or printer with a black-ink ribbon.

As mentioned in the introduction to this book, word-processing files containing the Articles and all of the tear-out forms included at the back of this book are available from Nolo's Website. If you don't want to fill in the Articles and other forms with a typewriter, you can download them using the Internet. See the Introduction to this book for more information.

ARTICLES OF INCORPORATION

OF

___(NAME OF CORPORATION)___

ONE: The name of this corporation is __(name of corporation)__.❶

TWO: The purpose of this corporation is to engage in any lawful act or activity for which a corporation may be organized under the General Corporation Law of California other than the banking business, the trust company business or the practice of a profession permitted to be incorporated by the California Corporations Code.

THREE: The name and address in this state of the corporation's initial agent for service of process is:__(name and address of initial agent)__.❷

FOUR: This corporation is authorized to issue only one class of shares of stock, which shall be designated common stock. The total number of shares it is authorized to issue is __(number of shares)__ shares.❸

FIVE: The names and addresses of the persons who are appointed to act as the initial directors of this corporation are:❹

Name   Address

_____   _____

_____   _____

_____   _____

_____   _____

_____   _____

SIX: The liability of the directors of the corporation for monetary damages shall be eliminated to the fullest extent permissible under California law.❺

SEVEN: The corporation is authorized to indemnify the directors and officers of the corporation to the fullest extent permissible under California law.❺

IN WITNESS WHEREOF, the undersigned, being all the persons named above as the initial directors, have executed these Articles of Incorporation.❻

DATED: _____ _____

_____

_____

_____

_____

_____

The undersigned, being all the persons named above as the initial directors, declare that they are the persons who executed the foregoing Articles of Incorporation, which execution is their act and deed.❻

DATED _____ _____

_____

_____

_____

_____

_____

Special Instructions

❶ Indicate the name of the corporation in the blanks in the heading and in Article ONE. Make sure this exact name is your final choice for a corporate name and that you have checked its availability for corporate use and/or reserved it with the Secretary of State as discussed in Chapter 2.

❷ Indicate the name and address (business or residence) of the corporation's initial agent for service of process. This address must be a street address, not a P.O. Box, within California. The initial agent for service of process is the person whom you designate to receive legal documents for the corporation. Most incorporators will give the name of one of the directors and the principal office of the corporation as the name and address of the corporation's initial agent.

❸ Indicate the number of authorized shares of the corporation. The traditional longhand method is to first spell out the number, then indicate the figure in parentheses, e.g., "ONE HUNDRED THOUSAND (100,000), but you do not need to be so formal, and can simply insert a number, such as 100,000.

Authorized shares are simply those that the corporation can sell to shareholders, after which they are referred to as "issued shares." There is no magic formula for computing the exact number of authorized shares you should specify—you can authorize as many or as few shares as you wish. However, the number of authorized shares you specify must, of course, be large enough to cover your initial stock issuance. To be sure it is, you may wish to skip ahead to the instructions for preparing the "Authorization of Issuance of Shares" resolution in the Minutes of the First Board Meeting in Chapter 5, Section A. After determining the actual number of initial shares you will issue to all shareholders, and adding a little extra to allow for the future issuance of additional shares (see "You May Want to Authorize Extra Shares in Your Articles" below), type the appropriate number here.

💡 YOU MAY WANT TO AUTHORIZE EXTRA SHARES IN YOUR ARTICLES

Authorizing additional shares in your Articles—in an amount greater than the actual amount you plan to initially issue—can be helpful if in the future you wish to implement a stock-bonus or -option plan, wish to bring new shareholders on board or simply wish to issue additional shares to your existing shareholders. If you don't authorize extra shares in your Articles now, and later decide to issue additional shares to new or existing shareholders, you will have to prepare an amendment to your Articles of Incorporation that increases the total authorized number of shares and then file the amendment with the California Secretary of State's office. In other words, if you add extra shares now as a cushion to cover your future stock needs, you can avoid this Articles amendment procedure later.

IF YOU WANT TO ISSUE SPECIAL CLASSES OF STOCK

Notice that Article FOUR authorizes the issuance of one class of shares, designated as "common stock." This means that all shares issued by the corporation are shares with equal voting, dividend, liquidation and other rights (all shareholders can vote, and they share in dividends and liquidation assets proportionate to share holdings, but no shareholder is granted a preference in receiving dividends or liquidation assets before other shareholders). A one-class stock structure should be sufficient for most smaller corporations, at least to start.

If you wish to establish one or more special classes of shares with special voting, dividend, liquidation or other rights, you will need to change Article FOUR, and add language that specifies the rights and restrictions associated with each class of shares. For a simple two-class stock structure, this is easy to do. For example, just change Article FOUR to read: *"This corporation is authorized to issue 100,000 Class A voting shares and 50,000 Class B nonvoting shares."* But for more complicated stock structures, such as one that includes a class with special restrictions on the transfer of shares (for example, a special class of stock-bonus shares that can be repurchased by the corporation when a shareholder leaves the employ of the corporation) or a class with special dividend or asset participation rights, you will need to do further research or consult a lawyer or tax advisor for the exact language to use to set up each class of shares. Typically, special classes of this sort are used when banks, investors or others wish to extend credit or provide extra capital in return for special voting, dividend or stock conversion rights in a corporation, and these outside entities often will provide language of their own for you to use to authorize and implement a special multitiered stock structure (again, you will have to change Article FOUR to add this special language to your Articles).

❹ Indicate the full name(s) and addresses(es) (business or residence) of your initial director(s).

Remember from Chapter 1: the general rule is that a California corporation must have at least three directors. However, if you will have only two shareholders, you may have only two directors; if you will have only one shareholder, you can have one director or two directors. Of course, you can exceed the minimum number of directors when setting up your corporation if you wish—for example, a one-shareholder corporation can have three or four directors.

❺ Article SIX uses the language contained in Section 204.5 of the California Corporations Code to eliminate the personal liability of directors for monetary damages to the fullest extent permissible under California law. This is a specialized article that can be helpful in limiting the personal liability of directors in shareholder derivative suits (suits brought by the corporation for breach of a director's duty of care to the corporation or stockholders).

Article SEVEN uses language contained in Section 317(g) of the California Corporations Code to allow the corporation to provide indemnification for the directors and officers beyond the limits expressly permitted by other subsections of Section 317. (Indemnification is the legal term for payment by the corporation of legal expenses, judgments, settlements, fines and other payments incurred by corporate directors and officers because of their official acts or omissions while serving the corporation.) This article really does very little except allow the corporation to adopt special indemnification provisions in its Bylaws (the basic Bylaws included with this book does not contain special indemnification language). If either of these areas is important to you, and you want to learn more, see *How to Form a California Corporation*, by Anthony Mancuso (Nolo Press), or consult your lawyer.

❻ There are two sets of date and signature lines that you must fill out at the bottom of your Articles. Although the second set of signatures seem redundant, their inclusion is a requirement of California law. Have each person named as initial director in Article FIVE date and sign the Articles in both places shown. Make sure that the signed and typed name(s) correspond(s) exactly to the name(s) as given in Article FIVE. Use a black-ink pen when signing your Articles—the Secretary of State must be able to photocopy your original Articles.

B. Prepare the Cover Letter for Filing Articles

➡ **IF YOU FILE ARTICLES IN PERSON**

If you file your Articles in person at one of the offices of the Secretary of State (Fresno, Los Angeles, Sacramento, San Diego or San Francisco), you do not need to prepare this letter. There is an additional $15 fee for filing Articles in person, as explained in Section C below. If you are interested in filing in person, skip to Section C below.

You need to include a cover letter when mailing your Articles to the California Secretary of State for filing. We include a sample letter in the Appendix of this book. Fill in this tear-out cover letter from the Appendix as you follow the sample cover letter and special instructions below.

✔ The parenthetical blanks, i.e., " (information) ," indicate information that you must complete on the tear-out form.

✔ Each circled number (e.g., ❶) refers to a special instruction that provides specific information to help you complete an item.

✔ Fill in the tear-out form using a typewriter or printer with a black-ink ribbon.

COVER LETTER FOR FILING ARTICLES

(type name and address of initial director/incorporator here) ❶

Secretary of State
Corporate Filing and Services Division
1500 11th Street
Sacramento, CA 95814

Secretary of State:
I enclose an original and ___(number)___ ❷ copies of the proposed Articles of Incorporation for ___(proposed name of corporation)___ .
[This corporate name was reserved with your office pursuant to Certificate of Registration #_____.] ❸
Also enclosed is a check/money order in payment of the following fees:

Prepaid Minimum Franchise Tax	$600/$800
(CIRCLE EITHER $600 OR $800)	
Filing Articles of Incorporation	$100
Comparing and certifying __ copies	$_____
(TWO COPIES CERTIFIED FOR FREE)	
TOTAL	$_____ ❹

If the $600 amount is circled above, the undersigned certifies on behalf of the proposed corporation that the proposed corporation is a "qualified new corporation" eligible to pay the reduced $600 prepaid minimum franchise tax upon incorporation under Revenue and Taxation Code Section 23221.
Please file the original Articles, and return the certified copies to me at the above address.

_____ ❺

    (type the name of the initial   ,Incorporator
    director/incorporator here)

Special Instructions

❶ Insert the name and address of the initial director who will sign the cover letter. If you reserved your corporate name, this person should be the same individual who obtained the corporate name reservation on behalf of the corporation (Chapter 2, Section E).

❷ Insert the number of copies you are including for certification with your original Articles. Certification means the Secretary of State compares the original to the copy, then file-stamps (stamps with the date and time) the copy and includes a gold seal showing certification by the state. Normally, two certified copies are sufficient: one for inclusion in the Minutes of the First Board Meeting and one as an extra copy. All copies should be legible with good contrast. Do not use rivet-type fasteners in putting your copies or original Articles together—use staples instead. Next, insert the proposed name of your corporation at the end of the first paragraph.

IF YOU RETYPE OR REFORMAT YOUR ARTICLES

Use letter-size (8 1/2" x 11") paper, type on one side of the paper only, and leave a three-inch square space in the upper right-hand corner of the first page of the Articles for the Secretary of State's file stamp.

❸ If you reserved a corporate name (see Chapter 2, Section E), type the optional bracketed sentence shown above (*"This corporate name was reserved with your office pursuant to Certificate of Registration #_____."*) under the first paragraph, specifying your corporate name reservation number at the end of the sentence.

❹ Compute the fees you must pay to file your Articles. These fees include:
- First year minimum franchise tax payment—the standard amount is $800, but some corporations are eligible to pay a reduced minimum first-year franchise tax of $600 as explained below.
- $100 filing fee

- Cost of certified copies. The Secretary will compare and certify two copies of the Articles for free. If you include more than two copies, they will be certified at an extra cost of $8 each.

DO YOU QUALIFY FOR A REDUCED $600 FIRST-YEAR MINIMUM FRANCHISE TAX?

If your corporation expects to have gross receipts of less than $1 million in your first tax year, and expects to have a California income-tax liability of $800 or less for this first tax year (use the California franchise tax rate of 8.84% to estimate your first year taxes), it is eligible to pay a reduced minimum tax of $600 when filing its Articles. A corporation that expects 50% or more of its initial shares of stock to be owned by another corporation is not eligible for this reduced $600 tax payment. If your tax liability turns out to be more than $800 for your first tax year and you pay the reduced amount of $600 when filing your Articles, you will be required to pay $200 to the Franchise Tax Board at the end of your first tax year.

REDUCED SECOND-YEAR MINIMUM TAX FOR SOME SMALLER CORPORATIONS

For second and future tax years, all corporations must pay a minimum franchise tax payment to the California Franchise Tax Board. Be forewarned: The minimum payment for your corporation's second tax year comes during your first quarter of corporate operations, right after you incorporate (because California requires you to prepay estimated franchise taxes during, not after, the tax year for which they are due). This means that you will have to make another minimum franchise tax payment soon after you file your Articles.

Section 23153 of the California Revenue and Taxation Code provides a tax break for qualified corporations—it allows them to pay $500, instead of $800, as a minimum tax for their second tax year (this reduces the minimum franchise tax payment that must be made during your first tax year shortly after you incorporate). Of course, if you expect to pay more than $500 in actual taxes by the end of your second tax year, this break ultimately will not save you any money (you'll just have to pay the difference—$300—at the end of the second year). To qualify for this lower second-tax-year minimum tax, the corporation must not have operated as a sole proprietorship, partnership or any other type of business prior to its incorporation. Also, gross receipts of the corporation for the second tax year must be expected to be less than $1 million.

Circle the amount of franchise tax you are including in your fee check—either the $600 or the $800 amount in the "prepaid minimum franchise tax" line in the list of fees (in case you circle the $600 amount, the letter includes a paragraph that says you are eligible under the California Revenue and Taxation code for the reduced $600 first-year minimum franchise tax). Then insert the number of copies you are including for certification and the amount enclosed for such certification. If you are enclosing only two copies for certification, insert "0" as the amount included for certification. Finally, add up the total amount of fees

---

AVOIDING FIRST-YEAR TAX PAYMENTS

You may be able to avoid franchise tax payments for your first tax year by delaying the filing of your Articles until a specific date in your second tax year (and thus avoid being taxed for a short first tax year). California law (Corporations Code §110) allows you to request a delayed filing date for your Articles as long as this date is no more than 90 days from the date the Secretary of State receives your Articles. If you wish to do this, change the last paragraph in the cover letter by adding a specific date on which the Articles should be filed.

Example: If your corporate tax year will run from January 1 to December 31 (you select a calendar tax year), and you mail your Articles to the Secretary of State at the beginning of December 2002, you can ask in your cover letter that the Articles be filed on January 1st, 2003. To do this, change the last paragraph in the cover letter to read as follows: "Please file the original Articles on January 1, 2003, and return the certified copies to me at the above address." (We recommend you underline or place in boldface type the delayed filing date to call attention to this part of your cover letter). By doing this you avoid being taxed for the first short tax year that would otherwise occur in 2002, which would start on the date your Articles were received by the Secretary of State and end on December 31, 2002.

There is a another way to avoid paying franchise taxes for a short first tax year: If your corporation has a first tax year of less than one-half month and the corporation is inactive during this period, then a state franchise-tax return is not required, and no franchise taxes are owed for the first tax year.

Example: If a corporation selects a calendar tax year and files its Articles on December 20th, 2002, as long as the corporation is inactive during this period, it owes no franchise taxes for the first short tax year of December 20th–31, 2002. In other words, the prepaid first-year minimum franchise-tax payment made with the filing of the Articles will be applied to the corporation's second tax year, starting on January 1, 2003.

The maximum duration of this one-half month period varies depending upon the length of the month involved. Specifically, FTB rules say that a short tax year will be ignored (meaning no first-year tax payment will be owed) if, in the case of a 28-day month, the Articles were filed on the 15th of the month or later; if Articles were filed during a 29- or 30-day month, they must have been filed on the 16th or later; and for a 31-day month, on the 17th or later. Call the Franchise Tax Board in Sacramento if you want to establish a short first tax year of less than one-half month to be sure these special rules are current at the time you incorporate.

and insert it in the last line of the fee list. If you are not eligible to pay the reduced $600 minimum tax amount and enclose two copies of the Articles for certification, the total fee amount is $900. Total fees are $700 if you are eligible for the reduced first-year minimum tax of $600 and you enclose two copies of the Articles for certification.

❺ Have the initial director whose name and address you inserted at the top of the letter sign the letter.

C. File Your Articles of Incorporation

Filing your Articles is a formality—the Secretary of State will file your papers if they conform to law and the proper fees are paid.

To file your Articles by mail, send the original form you filled out, the number of copies you wish to have certified, the cover letter and a check or money order for the total fees, payable to the "California Secretary of State." Send these papers to the Sacramento office of the Secretary of State shown in the heading of the cover letter. It normally takes ten business days or so for your Articles to be filed and returned to you by mail (it can take longer during busy filing periods, so you may need to be patient). Of course, if you request a delayed filing date for your Articles, expect to wait until after this delayed date to receive certified copies of your Articles from the Secretary of State.

How to File Your Articles in Person

You may file your Articles in person at any office of the Secretary of State (see below). There is an additional $15 special handling fee for filing your Articles in person. This fee is retained by the clerk if your Articles are rejected (for example, if your proposed corporate name is unavailable for your use). If you file your Articles in person at an office other than the main Sacramento office, you must provide the filing clerk with an extra signed copy of your Articles (this

copy is in addition to the two copies provided for certification, which are returned to you). The additional copy is forwarded by the local office to the Sacramento office of the Secretary of State. Here are the Secretary of State office addresses and phone numbers :

Fresno
2497 West Shaw, Suite 101
Fresno, CA 93711
209-243-2100

Los Angeles
300 South Spring Street, Room 12513
Los Angeles, CA 90013-1233
213-897-3062

Sacramento
1500 11th Street
Sacramento, CA 95814
916-653-6814

San Diego
1350 Front Street, Suite 2060
San Diego, CA 92101-3690
619-525-4113

San Francisco
235 Montgomery Street, Suite 725
San Francisco, CA 94104
415-439-6959

SET UP A CORPORATE RECORDS BINDER

You will need a corporate records binder to keep in an orderly fashion all your papers—your Articles, Bylaws and minutes (of the First Board Meeting, as well as ongoing director and shareholder meetings), a register containing the names and addresses of your shareholders, stock certificates and stubs, and other corporate papers such as loan documents. Setting up and maintaining a neat, well-organized records binder is one of your corporation's most important tasks—not only will it serve as a repository for corporate documents, it will act as a formal "paper trail" documenting organizational and ongoing corporate formalities. You should keep your corporate records binder at the principal office of your corporation at all times.

To set up a corporate records binder, you can simply place all of your incorporation documents in a three-ring binder. If you prefer, however, you can order a corporate records kit from Nolo Press by completing one of the order forms contained at the back of this book. Each Nolo Advantage™ Records Kit includes:

- A *Corporate Records Binder* with index dividers for Articles of Incorporation, Bylaws, Minutes and Stock Certificates;
- Twenty lithographed green *Stock Certificates* with the name and state of formation of your corporation printed on the face of each certificate;
- A printed *Stock Certificate Legend* on each certificate that says your shares have not been registered under the federal or state securities laws. This legend is not required legally, but it is a precaution you may want to take to help secure a stock issuance exemption (see Chapter 1, Section C);
- *Share Register* and *Transfer Ledger* pages to keep a consolidated record of the names and addresses of your shareholders, and the dates of issuance, surrender and transfer of your corporation's shares;
- Special instructions for using each section of the corporate records binder.

A higher-priced kit, called the Portfolio Corporate Records Kit, is also available through Nolo Press, and is advertised at the back of this book. In addition to a corporate records binder, this kit includes a metal Corporate Seal designed to emboss your corporate name and year of incorporation on corporate documents. A corporate seal is not legally required, but comes in handy to formalize stock certificates and other important corporate documents.

 WAIT UNTIL YOUR ARTICLES ARE FILED BEFORE ORDERING A CORPORATE KIT

We recommend you wait until you receive the certified copies of your filed Articles from the Secretary of State's office before you purchase a corporate records book, printed certificates and/or a corporate seal. This way, you'll be sure that you really have set up a corporation and that you have the right to use your proposed corporate name before you pay for these materials. Of course, if you are committed to forming your corporation, you know that you will be filing your Articles before the close of the year, and you have reserved your proposed corporate name for your use, then you're probably safe in ordering a corporate records kit and related materials ahead of time. ■

CHAPTER 4

Prepare Corporate Bylaws

After you file your Articles your business corporation is a legal entity, but there are still a few important steps to take to complete the organization of your corporation. The first of these steps is to prepare Bylaws for your new corporation. Bylaws contain the ground rules for ongoing decisions and formalities, such as how and when to hold regular and special meetings of directors and shareholders and how many votes are necessary for board action. They also restate the fundamental statutory rules that apply to your corporation under the California Corporations Code. Your Bylaws are an internal document, which you file in your corporate records binder for future reference—you do not normally need to file a copy with any state agency.

A. Fill in the Bylaws

It's easy to prepare the Bylaws contained in the Appendix of this book. Although the Bylaws will be your longest organizational document, you will only have to fill in a few blanks. Fill in the Bylaws as you follow the sample form and instructions below. The Bylaws are a lengthy document, so, to save space, in the sample Bylaws below, we have excerpted only the Bylaw provisions that you must fill in.

✔ The parenthetical blanks, i.e., "_(information)_," indicate information that you must complete on the form.

✔ Each circled number (e.g., ❶) refers to a special instruction that provides specific information to help you complete an item. The special instructions immediately follow the sample form.

✔ Fill in the tear-out form using a typewriter or printer with a black-ink ribbon.

MAKING CHANGES TO BYLAWS

We considered several approaches to handling corporate formalities before settling on the provisions included in the Bylaws in the Appendix of this book. Ultimately, we decided to include minimal rules, such as the requirement for holding of an annual meeting of the board of directors, a majority quorum requirement for shareholders' meetings, and requirements for standard notice of meetings, even though these are not absolutely required under California law. On the other hand, we did not require a whole host of other formal rules (such as requiring special qualifications for directors and requiring an annual report to be prepared and sent to all shareholders each year), believing that most people who run small- and moderate-sized businesses wish to run their operations without layers of formal operating rules.

Most incorporators should feel that these Bylaws meet their minimum needs—please read them to see if you agree. If you wish to add to, or otherwise modify, the Bylaws we provide—especially if you want to dispense with the minimal level of formality we provide—please check (or have a lawyer check) your changes against the General Corporation Law (this is the law that applies to business corporations, and is found in Sections 100 through 2319 of the California Corporations Code). In most cases the law allows you to specify your own rules, but there are some areas of corporate decision-making and operations that must follow mandatory rules set out in the General Corporation Law.

 LOOK UP THE GENERAL CORPORATION LAW ON THE INTERNET

You can read one or more sections of the General Corporation Law online by pointing your browser to "http://www.leginfo.ca.gov/calaw.html." Then click the "Corporations Code" box, fill in the search box with the desired code section number, and click the Search button.

BYLAWS
OF
_____(name of corporation)_____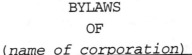

.
.
.

ARTICLE II
SHAREHOLDERS' MEETINGS

SECTION 1. PLACE OF MEETINGS

All meetings of the shareholders shall be held at the principal executive office of the corporation or at such other place as may be determined by the board of directors.

SECTION 2. ANNUAL MEETINGS

The annual meeting of the shareholders shall be held each year on ____(day, month and time of annual shareholders' meeting)__, ❷ at which time the shareholders shall elect a board of directors and transact any other proper business. If this date falls on a legal holiday, then the meeting shall be held on the following business day at the same hour.

.
.
.

ARTICLE III
DIRECTORS

SECTION 1. POWERS

Subject to any limitations in the Articles of Incorporation and to the provisions of the California Corporations Code, the business and affairs of the corporation shall be managed, and all corporate powers shall be exercised, by, or under the direction of, the board of directors.

SECTION 2. NUMBER

The authorized number of directors shall be ___(total number of directors who will serve on your board)__. ❸

After issuance of shares, this bylaw may only be amended by approval of a majority of the outstanding shares entitled to vote; provided, moreover, that a bylaw reducing the fixed number of directors to a number less than five (5) cannot be adopted unless in accordance with the additional requirements of Article IX of these Bylaws.

.

.

.

SECTION 8. QUORUM AND BOARD ACTION

A quorum for all meetings of the board of directors shall consist of _(number, or percentage of total number, of directors that will represent a quorum)_ ❹ of the authorized number of directors until changed by amendment to this article of these Bylaws.

Every act or decision done or made by a majority of the directors present at a meeting duly held at which a quorum is present is an act of the board, subject to the provisions of Section 310 (relating to the approval of contracts and transactions in which a director has a material financial interest); the provisions of Section 311 (designation of committees); and Section 317(e) (indemnification of directors) of the California Corporations Code. A meeting at which a quorum is initially present may continue to transact business notwithstanding the withdrawal of directors, if any action taken is approved by at least a majority of the required quorum for such meeting.

A majority of the directors present at a meeting may adjourn any meeting to another time and place, whether or not a quorum is present at the meeting.

.

.

.

CERTIFICATE

This is to certify that the foregoing is a true and correct copy of the Bylaws of the corporation named in the title thereto and that such Bylaws were duly adopted by the board of directors of the corporation on the date set forth below.

Dated: _____   _____ ❺

,Secretary

(impress corporate seal here) ❺

Special Instructions

❶ Heading: Type your corporate name in the heading of the Bylaws. Make sure the name shown here is the same as the name shown in the certified copies of your Articles returned from the Secretary of State's office.

❷ Article II, Section 2: Indicate the date and time of your annual shareholders' meeting—for example, "the last Friday in December at 9 a.m." or "June 15th at 1 o'clock PM." It's usually best to designate a fixed day (such as the second Monday of a particular month) rather than a date, to avoid having the meetings fall on a weekend.

Section 600 of the Corporations Code requires you to hold this annual meeting of shareholders to elect the board of directors. Your corporation's annual directors' meeting is automatically scheduled to be held immediately after this shareholders' meeting (see Article III, Section 7, in the Bylaws in the Appendix of this book). The newly elected (or re-elected) board members attend this subsequent board meeting.

The date of the corporation's shareholders' meeting is commonly set shortly before or after the close of the corporation's tax year (or tax-return filing date) so that the prior year's business can be reviewed and the coming year's business can be discussed and planned. Some directors set this date during the last month of the corporation's tax year so that the board of directors may, immediately following their election at the shareholders' meeting, make important year-end tax decisions (for example, fixing the corporation's liability for expenses, such as employee bonuses, that they wish to deduct in the current year and pay after the start of the next corporate tax year).

❸ Article III, Section 2: Indicate the authorized number of directors of your corporation—this is the total number of directors who will serve on your board, and should be the same as the number of initial directors named in your Articles (see Chapter 3, Section A). Remember: the general rule is that a California corporation must have at least three directors. However, a corporation with only two shareholders may have only two directors, and a one-shareholder corporation may have one or two directors. Of course, you may provide for more than the minimum number of directors required by law—for example, if you are the only shareholder in your corporation, you may wish to have your spouse serve as a second director to participate in management decisions.

❹ Article III, Section 8: Indicate the number, or the percentage of the total number, of directors who must be present at a directors' meeting to constitute a "quorum" so that business can be conducted. Typical responses are "a majority," "one-third," "two" and the like. Although the usual practice is to use the "majority" quorum, under California law you may provide that a quorum be as little as one-third the number of authorized directors, or two, whichever is larger. A one-person corporation, however, may (and will) provide for a one-director quorum.

Example: A four-director corporation, under the above minimum rules, may provide for a quorum of two, rather than a majority (which would be three directors). Applying these rules to a three-director corporation results in a quorum of two.

Whatever you decide, realize that this section of the Bylaws concerns the number of directors necessary for quorum, not the number of directors necessary to pass a vote. Action at a directors' meeting can be approved by the vote of a majority of directors present at a meeting at which a quorum is present. For example, if a six-director corporation requires a majority quorum, and a meeting is held at which a minimum quorum (four) is present, action can be taken by the vote of three directors, a majority of those present at the meeting.

❺ Do not date, sign or seal your Bylaws at the bottom of the last page at this time. The corporate Secretary will do this after you hold your First Meeting of the Board of Directors (as explained in the next chapter). (Although a seal is not required, if you have one, here is a good place to use it.)

That's all there is to preparing the Bylaws. Make a copy for approval by the board and signing by your corporate Secretary, as explained in the next chapter. ∎

C H A P T E R 5

Prepare Minutes of First Board Meeting

The next step, now that you have filed your Articles and prepared your Bylaws, is to prepare the Minutes of the First Meeting of the Board of Directors. After preparing your Minutes according to Section A below, you will actually hold a meeting as explained in Section B below. (It's a good idea to prepare your Minutes before the actual meeting, so you can follow the agenda they set during the meeting.)

The purpose of your Minutes is to document essential organizational actions taken by your board of directors, including:

- Adopting the Bylaws you created in Chapter 4.
- Specifying the principal office of the corporation.
- Appointing officers.
- Adopting an accounting period (also the tax year) for your corporation.
- Authorizing the issuance of the initial shares of stock of the corporation.
- If federal S corporation tax status is desired, approving this election.

A. Fill in the Minutes Form

Prepare your Minutes by filling in the blanks in the Minutes of the First Meeting of the Board of Directors form in the Appendix of this book as you follow the sample form and instructions below. There is nothing difficult here, but there are a number of questions that you must answer.

✔ The parenthetical blanks, i.e., " *(information)* ," indicate information that you must complete on the form.

✔ Each circled number (e.g., ❶) refers to a special instruction that provides specific information to help you complete an item. The special instructions immediately follow the sample form.

✔ Fill in the tear-out form using a typewriter or printer with a black-ink ribbon.

WAIVER OF NOTICE AND CONSENT TO HOLDING OF
FIRST MEETING OF BOARD OF DIRECTORS
OF
(name of corporation) ❶

We, the undersigned, being all the directors of _(name of corporation)_ , ❶ a California corporation, hereby waive notice of the first meeting of the board of directors of the corporation and consent to the holding of said meeting at _(address of meeting)_ , on _(date of meeting)_ , at _(time of meeting)_ ❶ and consent to the transaction of any and all business by the directors at the meeting, including, without limitation, the adoption of Bylaws, the appointment of officers, the selection of the corporation's accounting period, the designation of the principal executive office of the corporation, the selection of the place where the corporation's bank accounts will be maintained, and the authorization of the sale and issuance of the initial shares of stock of the corporation.

DATED: _____ ❶

_____
(signature of director)
(type name of director)   , Director

_____
(signature of director)
(type name of director)   , Director

_____
(signature of director)
(type name of director)   , Director ❶

MINUTES OF FIRST MEETING OF THE BOARD OF DIRECTORS
OF
(name of corporation) ❷

The board of directors of _(name of corporation)_ ❷ held its first meeting at _(address of meeting)_, on _(date of meeting)_, at _(time of meeting)_.❷

The following directors, if marked as present next to their names, were in attendance at the meeting and constituted a quorum of the full board:

(name of director)   [ ] Present [ ] Absent

(name of director)   [ ] Present [ ] Absent

(name of director)   [ ] Present [ ] Absent ❸

On motion and by unanimous vote,_(name of director)_ ❹ was elected temporary chairperson and then presided over the meeting. _(name of director)_ ❹ was elected temporary secretary of the meeting.

The chairperson announced that the meeting was held pursuant to written waiver of notice and consent to holding of the meeting signed by each of the directors. Upon a motion duly made, seconded, and unanimously carried, it was resolved that the written waiver of notice and consent to holding of the meeting be made a part of the minutes of the meeting and placed in the corporation's records binder.

FILING OF ARTICLES OF INCORPORATION

The chairperson announced that the Articles of Incorporation of the corporation were filed with the California Secretary of State's office on _(date of filing of Articles)_ ❺ The chairperson then presented to the meeting a certified copy of the Articles showing such filing and the secretary was instructed to insert this copy in the corporation's records binder.

ADOPTION OF BYLAWS ❻

A proposed set of Bylaws of the corporation was then presented to the meeting for adoption. The Bylaws were considered and discussed and, upon motion duly made and seconded, it was unanimously

RESOLVED, that the Bylaws presented to this meeting be and hereby are adopted as the Bylaws of this corporation;

RESOLVED FURTHER, that the secretary of this corporation be and hereby is directed to execute a Certificate of Adoption of the Bylaws, to insert the Bylaws as so certified in the corporation's records binder and to see that a copy of the Bylaws, similarly certified, is kept at the corporation's principal executive office, as required by law.

APPOINTMENT OF OFFICERS

The chairperson then announced that the next item of business was the appointment of officers. Upon motion, the following persons were unanimously appointed to the following offices, at the annual salaries, if any, as determined at the meeting, shown to the right of their names:

President: _____*(name of officer)*_____ $ *(salary)*

Vice President: __*(name of officer)*_____ $ *(salary)*

Secretary: _____*(name of officer)*_____ $ *(salary)*

Treasurer: _____*(name of officer)*_____ $ *(salary)* ❼

Each officer who was present accepted his or her office. Thereafter, the President presided at the meeting as chairperson, and the Secretary acted as secretary.

ADOPTION OF CORPORATE SEAL ❽

The Secretary presented to the meeting for adoption a proposed form of seal of the corporation. Upon motion duly made and seconded, it was

RESOLVED, that the form of the corporate seal presented to this meeting be and hereby is adopted as the corporate seal of this corporation, and the secretary of this corporation is directed to place an impression thereof in the space directly next to this resolution.

ADOPTION OF STOCK CERTIFICATE ❾

The Secretary then presented to the meeting for adoption a proposed form of stock certificate for the corporation. Upon motion duly made and seconded, it was

RESOLVED, that the form of stock certificate presented to this meeting be and hereby is adopted for use by this corporation, and the secretary of this corporation is directed to annex a copy thereof to the minutes of this meeting.

SELECTION OF ACCOUNTING PERIOD ❿

The chairperson informed the board that the next order of business was the selection of the accounting period of the corporation. After discussion and upon motion duly made and seconded, it was

RESOLVED, that the accounting period of this corporation shall end on _(ending date of the accounting period of the corporation)_ of each year.

LOCATION OF PRINCIPAL EXECUTIVE OFFICE

After discussion as to the exact location of the corporation's principal executive office, upon motion duly made and seconded, it was

RESOLVED, that the principal executive office of this corporation shall be located at _(address, including city, county and state of principal executive office)_. ⓫

DESIGNATION OF BANK ACCOUNTS

The chairperson recommended that the corporation open a bank account with _(name of bank and branch office)_. ⓬ Upon motion duly made and seconded, it was

RESOLVED, that the funds of this corporation shall be deposited with the bank and branch office indicated just above.

RESOLVED FURTHER, that the Treasurer of this corporation is hereby authorized and directed to establish an account with said bank and to deposit the funds of this corporation therein.

RESOLVED FURTHER, that any officer, employee or agent of this corporation is hereby authorized to endorse checks, drafts or other evidences of indebtedness made payable to this corporation, but only for the purpose of deposit.

RESOLVED FURTHER, that all checks, drafts and other instruments obligating this corporation to pay money shall be signed on behalf of this corporation by any _(number)_ ⓬ of the following:

(name of person authorized to sign checks)

(name of person authorized to sign checks)

(name of person authorized to sign checks) ⓬

RESOLVED FURTHER, that said bank is hereby authorized to honor and pay any and all checks and drafts of this corporation signed as provided herein.

RESOLVED FURTHER, that the authority hereby conferred shall remain in force until revoked by the board of directors of this corporation and until written notice of such revocation shall have been received by said bank.

RESOLVED FURTHER, that the secretary of this corporation be and is hereby authorized to certify as to the continuing authority of these resolutions, the persons authorized to sign on behalf of this corporation and the adoption of said bank's standard form of resolution, provided that said form does not vary materially from the terms of the foregoing resolutions.

PAYMENT AND DEDUCTION OF ORGANIZATIONAL EXPENSES ⑬

The board next considered the question of paying the expenses incurred in the formation of this corporation. A motion was made, seconded and unanimously approved, and it was

RESOLVED, that the President and the Treasurer of this corporation are authorized and empowered to pay all reasonable and proper expenses incurred in connection with the organization of the corporation, including, among others, filing, licensing and attorney's and accountant's fees, and to reimburse any persons making any such disbursements for the corporation, and it was

FURTHER RESOLVED, that the Treasurer is authorized to elect to deduct on the first federal income-tax return of the corporation the foregoing expenditures ratably over a sixty-month period starting in the month the corporation begins its business, pursuant to, and to the extent permitted by, Section 248 of the Internal Revenue Code of 1986, as amended.

ELECTION OF FEDERAL S CORPORATION TAX TREATMENT ⑭

The board of directors next considered the advantages of electing to be taxed under the provisions of Subchapter S of the Internal Revenue Code of 1986, as amended. After discussion, upon motion duly made and seconded, it was unanimously

RESOLVED, that this corporation hereby elects to be treated as a Small Business Corporation for federal income tax purposes under Subchapter S of the Internal Revenue Code of 1986, as amended.

RESOLVED FURTHER, that the officers of this corporation take all actions necessary and proper to effectuate the foregoing resolution, including, among other things, obtaining the re_____ ____nsents from the shareholders of this corporation and ex_____ _____ _____ appropriate forms with the Internal Revenue _____ _____ _____ecified by law.

SECTION 1244 STOCK ⓯

The b_____ _____ _____ity of qualifying the stock of this corporati_____ _____d in Section 1244 of the Internal Revenue C_____ _____ganizing and managing the corporati_____ _____orporation as defined in that section. _____ _____ it was unanimously

RESOLV_____ _____corporation are, subject to the requiremen_____ _____fornia and any other applicable securities _____ _____shares of stock in return for the receip_____ _____d other property, as a contributi_____ _____lus, which does not exceed $1,000,000

RESOLVE_____ _____ of shares shall be conducted in complia_____ _____poration and its shareholders may obtain _____ _____

_____ of that section.

RESOLVED FURT____ _____ ____cers of the corporation are directed to maintain such records as are necessary pursuant to Section 1244 so that any shareholder who experiences a loss on the transfer of shares of stock of the corporation may determine whether he or she qualifies for ordinary loss deduction treatment on his or her individual income-tax return.

AUTHORIZATION OF ISSUANCE OF SHARES

The board of directors next took up the matter of the sale and issuance of stock to provide capital for the corporation. Upon motion duly made and seconded, it was unanimously

RESOLVED, that the corporation sell and issue the following number of its authorized common shares to the following persons, in the amounts and for the consideration set forth to the right of their names below. The board also hereby determines that the fair value to the corporation of any consideration for such shares issued other than for money is as set forth below: ⓰

Although the Nabats are feeling positive about their son's dream finally coming true, they've cut off his funding. "I finally said to him, 'It's enough,'" said Gene Nabat. Craig Nabat's story is not that unusual. Most small businesses and new product launches are self-funded with the help of friends and family members. Here are Craig Nabat's tips for fellow inventors:

1. Read Napoleon Hill's "Think and Grow Rich."
2. Write a business plan that's a life plan. "If I didn't have a plan during this process, I'd be lost."
3. Don't give up no matter what.
4. Don't listen to what other people say, but tell many people about your plans.
5. Don't worry about where you are going to get the money. "If you stick with something long enough, you'll eventually find the money to do it."

Reporting by Robin Wallace. Jane Applegate is a syndicated columnist and author of "201 Great Ideas for Your Small Business." For more small-business resources, visit jane@janeapplegate.com.

Name	Number of Shares	Consideration	Fair Value
_____	_____	_____	$_____
_____	_____	_____	$_____
_____	_____	_____	$_____
_____	_____	_____	$_____
_____	_____	_____	$_____
_____	_____	_____	$_____
_____	_____	_____	$_____
_____	_____	_____	$_____

RESOLVED FURTHER, that these shares shall be sold and issued by this corporation strictly in accordance with the terms of the exemption from qualification of these shares as provided for in Section 25102(f) of the California Corporations Code.

RESOLVED FURTHER, that the appropriate officers of this corporation are hereby authorized and directed to take such actions and execute such documents as they may deem necessary or appropriate to effectuate the sale and issuance of such shares for such consideration.

Since there was no further business to come before the meeting, upon motion duly made and seconded, the meeting was adjourned.

_____

       , Secretary ❶⓻

Special Instructions

❶ Waiver of Notice and Consent to Holding of First Meeting of Board of Directors: This form is included as the first page of the Minutes. It is necessary to dispense with formal director notice requirements that apply to special board meetings (the first meeting of the board is a special board meeting). Indicate the name of your corporation in the heading and in the first blank of the first paragraph. Indicate the address, date and time of your first directors' meeting. Normally, you will show the address of the corporation here as the place of your board meeting. Insert the date of signing at the end of the waiver page, then have each initial director named in the Articles sign the form.

HAVE AN IN-PERSON MEETING

We think it's wise for your first meeting to be more than just a "paper" meeting. In other words, if you have more than one director, you should actually sit down with the other directors at the place, date and time indicated here to review and agree to the provisions in your completed Minutes.

❷ **Title Page of Minutes:** The next page of your Minutes contains the title of the document and begins by reciting the facts necessary for you to hold your meeting, repeating the name of your corporation and the address, date and time of the meeting given above. Fill in these five blanks as explained just above.

❸ **Present and Absent Directors:** Show the names of all your directors in these blanks. Check the appropriate box to the right of each name to show whether each director will be present at, or absent from, the first board meeting. Although we suggest that all of your directors be present at your first meeting, only a quorum of the board (as specified in Article III, Section 8, of your Bylaws) actually need attend this meeting. And, of course, if you are forming a closely held corporation and wish to approve your Minutes on paper only (without having to hold a real meeting), simply show that all initial directors are in attendance at this "paper" meeting. In this case, of course, we

assume that you have made sure that all initial directors are in agreement on the matters approved in these Minutes.

❹ **Designation of Temporary Chairperson and Secretary:** These blanks relate to a minor, but necessary, formality. Since you have not yet elected officers, these blanks show the names of the directors you name as temporary chairperson and secretary of your first meeting (after the first meeting, the corporate President and Secretary normally serve in these capacities). Type the name of one of your initial directors as your temporary chairperson in the first blank, and insert the name of another director as your temporary secretary in the second. If your corporation has only one initial director, you will, naturally, enter this person's name in both blanks.

❺ **Filing of Articles of Incorporation:** This is the first resolution of your Minutes and appears just after the introductory material on your title page. This resolution serves as a formal record of the date of filing of your Articles of Incorporation, and indicates the first day of the legal existence of your corporation. Insert in this blank the date on which your Articles were filed by the Secretary of State—this is not the date you sent the Articles, but the "endorsed-filed" date stamped on the first page of the certified copies of your Articles of Incorporation returned by the Secretary of State.

❻ **Adoption of Bylaws:** This resolution is included in your Minutes to show the formal adoption of your Bylaws by the directors. The Bylaws require you to keep your corporate records binder (and a copy of your Bylaws) at the principal executive office of the corporation. You will establish the location of this office in a separate resolution, as discussed below in special instruction ⓫.

❼ **Appointment of Officers:** This resolution is included for the appointment of the officers of the corporation by the board and for board authorization of any officer salaries the directors feel are appropriate. When filling in these blanks, remember the following points:
• Under California law, you must fill the offices of President, Secretary and Treasurer (the latter is

referred to in the California Corporations Code as the "Chief Financial Officer").

- You are not required to elect a Vice President, or any additional officers, although many directors will wish to do so.

- One person may be elected to all, or any number of, these officer positions. For example, in a one-person corporation, the one shareholder and director will be elected as President, Secretary and Treasurer (and Vice President, if this person wants to add this optional title to her name).

Example: Joan, Gary and Matthew form their own corporation. Since it's really Joan's business (her spouse Gary and her brother Matthew are simply investing as shareholders), Joan fills the officer positions of President, Secretary and Treasurer.

- An officer need not be a director or shareholder in your corporation (although, for small corporations, the officer usually will be both).

- For all the officers, filling in the salary blank is optional. Specifically, many corporations will not wish to provide for officer salaries—and will not fill in these blanks—because these individuals will actively work for the corporation and will not be paid a separate salary as an officer, per se, but in return for filling some other position related to the particular business of the corporation.

Example: Betty Bidecker is a 75% shareholder and the President and Treasurer of her incorporated software publishing company. Bix Bidecker, her spouse, is a 25% shareholder and the Vice President and Secretary of the corporation. Rather than being paid for serving in any officer capacity, both are paid annual salaries as executive employees of the corporation: Betty as the Publisher, Bix as the Associate Publisher.

- If you do provide for officer salaries, remember, salaries should be reasonable in view of the actual duties performed by the officer and should be comparable to compensation paid for similar skills in similar businesses (if an officer is excessively overpaid, the IRS may treat the excess salary as a nondeductible payment of a dividend by the cor-

poration to the shareholder-employee). Don't be overly concerned here: If you are active in your business and can afford to pay yourself a large salary because of the profitability of your corporation, your salary will most likely be reasonable in view of your material participation in your corporation's productivity and, generally, in view of the trend towards paying higher corporate salaries in most key corporate positions these days.

❽ Adoption of Corporate Seal: This resolution is included in your Minutes in case you wish to order and use a corporate seal (see corporate records kit order pages at the back of this book). If you have ordered a seal, stamp or impress the corporate seal in the space provided to the right of this resolution. A corporate seal is not legally necessary, however, and if you have not obtained one, just leave the space to the right of this resolution blank.

❾ Adoption of Stock Certificate: This resolution is included in your Minutes to show acceptance of the form of stock certificate you will use—either the tear-out certificates included in the Appendix in the back of this book or those which you have purchased on your own (perhaps as part of one of the corporate records kits available from or through Nolo Press—see order information at the back of this book). To show approval of your stock certificate, attach a certificate, marked as a "Specimen," to your completed Minutes.

❿ Selection of Accounting Period: This resolution allows you to specify the accounting period (also the tax year) of your corporation. You should select this period with the help of your tax advisor. In the blank, insert the date (month and day) of the end of your corporation's accounting period. For example, if you choose a calendar year accounting period for your corporation, insert the ending date as "December 31."

Realize that the California Franchise Tax Board and the IRS look to your initial corporate tax returns to determine the actual ending date of your corporate tax year and accounting period: If your first corporate tax returns are submitted for a period ending on July 30th, this date will be taken as the end date of your corporate tax year, and also will fix the ending date of your corporation's accounting period. After you file your initial corporate returns, you need the consent of the IRS and the California Franchise Tax Board to change your tax year (and the corporation's associated accounting period).

⓫ Location of Principal Executive Office: This resolution allows you to formally specify the "principal executive office" of your corporation. This is a term used in the Corporations Code to indicate the legal address of the corporation. We expect you to indicate your corporation's principal place of business—the street address where all or most of your corporation's business is carried out—as its principal executive office. Although not legally required, most corporations will indicate a principal executive office within California. Insert the street address, including the city, county and state, of the principal executive office of your corporation in the blank.

⓬ Designation of Bank Accounts: This resolution authorizes the opening of the corporation's bank account(s) with one or more banks, and shows the names of individuals authorized to sign corporate checks and the number of signatures required on them. Typically, you will also have to fill out a separate bank account authorization form provided by your bank.

YOU MAY NEED AN EMPLOYER ID NUMBER

Banks customarily require your corporation to have a federal employer identification number. This number is obtained by filing Form SS-4 with the IRS. All corporations who hire employees will also need to obtain a state employer number and make deposits of state and federal withholding and employment taxes with an authorized bank.

Type the name(s) of the bank(s) and branch office(s) where the corporation will maintain its accounts in the blank in the first paragraph. In the fifth paragraph, insert the number of individual signatures that will be required on each corporate check. For example, if you wish to require your President and

Secretary to sign all corporate checks, type "two" in this blank. Beneath the fifth paragraph, type the names of individuals who are authorized to sign checks on behalf of your corporation. For example, if you only require one authorized signature on corporate checks, you may wish to allow either your corporate Treasurer (who will normally sign checks) or your President (when necessary) to sign corporate checks. Generally, you will show the name of one or more officers or key employees (such as your salaried in-house bookkeeper) here.

⓭ Payment and Deduction of Organizational Expenses: This resolution is optional, and is included on a separate Minutes page. If you do not wish to use this resolution, do not include this page in your completed Minutes. Many incorporators will wish to include this resolution in their minutes to allow the corporation to reimburse the incorporators for, and have the corporation pay and deduct over a period of time, the expenses incurred in organizing the corporation under Section 248 of the Internal Revenue Code—without a specific election to deduct these expenses over a specified period of time, such a deduction is normally not possible.

Note that you must implement this federal tax election by attaching a statement to your first federal corporate income-tax return indicating that you are choosing to amortize organizational expenses, providing a description of the expenses together with other required details. Check with your tax advisor for help in deciding whether to use this resolution and for help in preparing the statement to include with your initial corporate tax returns.

⓮ Election of Federal S Corporation Tax Treatment: This resolution is optional, and is also included on a separate page of the Minutes. If you do not wish to use this resolution, do not include this page in your completed Minutes. The basic requirements and effect of making this tax election are briefly discussed in Chapter 1, section B2. The decision to include this resolution in your Minutes involves several tax factors, not covered in this book.

Essentially, an S corporation is one that elects to have its profits, losses, credits and deductions pass-through to its shareholders—in other words, once this tax election is made (by filing IRS Form 2553), corporate profits are taxed to each of the shareholders at their individual income tax rates, not at corporate rates. In essence, making an S corporation tax election with the IRS and California Franchise Tax Board results in your corporation being treated very much like a partnership for federal and state income tax purposes state. But there are some important technical differences that you will want to explore with your tax advisor before deciding to make this tax election.

FOR MORE INFORMATION

See *IRS Publication 589, Tax Information on S Corporations* and *How to Form Your Own California Corporation*, by Anthony Mancuso (Nolo Press).

⑮ Section 1244 Stock Resolution: This resolution is optional and is included on a separate Minutes page. If you do not wish to use this resolution, do not include this page in your completed Minutes. Most shareholders will wish to have their stock treated as Section 1244 stock—this is a special designation under federal tax law that allows any future stock losses to be deductible as "ordinary" instead of "capital losses." This resolution simply reflects the intent of the directors to take advantage of the Section 1244 provisions later in the event the stock of the corporation becomes worthless or is sold at a loss. Adopting this corporate resolution is not one of the requirements under Section 1244.

To be eligible under Section 1244, you must meet Section 1244 requirements, including the maintenance of specific records and the filing of a timely statement with the IRS at the time of a future stock loss—see the sidebar "Section 1244 Stock Loss Treatment Requirements" for more information. Your tax advisor can help you estimate if your shareholders will qualify later for Section 1244 stock treatment in the event of a future stock loss, and can help you meet the record-keeping and filing requirements associated with this special tax treatment.

SECTION 1244 STOCK LOSS TREATMENT REQUIREMENTS

Under Section 1244 of the Internal Revenue Code, smaller corporations can provide shareholders with the benefit of treating losses from the sale, exchange or worthlessness of their stock as "ordinary" rather than "capital" losses on their individual federal tax returns, up to a maximum of $50,000 ($100,000 for a husband and wife filing a joint return) in each tax year. This is a definite advantage, since ordinary losses are fully deductible against individual income, whereas capital losses are only partially deductible (normally the latter can only be used to offset up to $3,000 of individual income in a given tax year). Stock issued by a corporation that qualifies for this federal ordinary loss treatment is known as Section 1244 stock. To qualify for Section 1244 stock treatment, the following requirements must be met:

- The shares must be issued for money or property (other than corporate securities). More than 50% of the corporation's gross receipts during the five tax years preceding the year in which the loss occurred must have been derived from sources other than royalties, dividends, interest, rents, annuities or gains from sales or exchanges in securities or stock.

- The corporation must be a "small business corporation" as defined in Section 1244 of the Internal Revenue Code. This means that the total amount of money or value of property received by the corporation for stock, as a contribution to capital and as paid-in surplus, cannot exceed $1 million.

- Only the original owner of stock is eligible to take a Section 1244 loss. If you transfer your shares to a family member during your life or the shares pass, through your will to heirs or through your living trust to beneficiaries at your death, the transferees, heirs and beneficiaries are not entitled to claim a Section 1244 loss.

- At the time of loss, the shareholder must submit a timely statement to the IRS electing to take an ordinary loss pursuant to Section 1244.

⓰ Authorization of Issuance of Shares: This resolution authorizes your corporation to issue its initial shares to your shareholders *after* the First Meeting of the Board of Directors (we call this resolution your "stock issuance resolution"). Adoption of this resolution does not result in the issuance of shares—you will actually issue shares as part of Chapter 6 below.

Before filling out this section of your Minutes, you have to decide how much you'll charge per share. All of your initial shares should be sold for the same price per share. For example, if someone pays the corporation $1,000 cash for ten shares (at $100 per share), then another person giving the corporation a machine worth $10,000 should receive 100 shares.

There is no "best price" for shares. Fixing a price per share is arbitrary. In the example just given, it would be just as easy and sensible to establish a price per share amount of $50 with each shareholder receiving a stock certificate representing twice as many shares. But note that the shareholders would not want to fix the price per share amount in this example at $65 per share, for instance—this would result in the issuance of certificates representing fractional shares (in the above example, the shareholder who paid $1,000 cash would have to receive 15.38 shares). Although issuing fractional shares is legally permissible, it is an unnecessarily complex method of issuing your shares.

After you've decided on a per-share price, fill in a line for each person (for joint shareholders of stock, such as a husband and wife, use one line for each pair of co-owners) who will buy initial shares of stock. On each line, show the following (you may need to devote more than one line to each shareholder, particularly if you wish to provide a more lengthy description of the payment for shares as explained below):

- the name of the shareholder (or joint shareholders)
- the number of shares to be issued to each shareholder (or pair of joint shareholders)
- a brief description of the "consideration" (legally, this word means "payment") to be made for the shares—for example, cash or a specific type of property, such as furniture, computer equipment, an automobile, or even intangible property, such as the assignment of a lease, patent, trademark or copyright
- the fair value of the payment made by each shareholder. "Fair value" is the term the California Corporations Code uses—essentially, it means the true market value of the property given by a shareholder, as determined by the board. In other words, show the amount of cash to be paid or the dollar value of any noncash payment to be made for the shares.

HOW TO AUTHORIZE THE ISSUANCE OF SHARES

- Make sure that the total number of shares to be issued to all shareholders as listed in the Minutes of the First Board Meeting is not greater than the number of shares authorized in Article FOUR of your Articles of Incorporation—Article FOUR places an upper limit on the number of shares that you can actually issue.

  Under California law, you may issue shares only for:
- cash
- tangible or intangible property actually received by the corporation
- debts cancelled (the cancellation of a note reflecting money owed by the corporation to the shareholder), and
- labor done or services actually rendered to the corporation, for its benefit or in its formation.

  You cannot issue shares in return for the promise of future services by a shareholder, nor can you issue shares in return for promissory notes (a promise by the shareholder to pay for the shares later), unless the promissory note is secured by collateral other than the shares themselves.
- As a matter of common sense, and to avoid unfairness or fraud, issue your shares for the same price per share to all initial shareholders. When accepting property other than cash in exchange for shares, make sure to place a fair value on the assets or other property or services being given in return for the shares. If you are transferring the assets of an existing business to your corporation in return for shares (in other words, you are incorporating a prior business), we suggest that you have an accountant or other qualified appraiser make a written determination of the value of these assets. You may also wish to have a balance sheet prepared for the prior business at the time of transfer, showing the assets and liabilities being transferred to your corporation. In all cases when issuing shares in return for property, be fair and realistic in your determination of the value of the property, particularly if you will be issuing shares in return for speculative or intangible property such as the goodwill of a business, copyrights, patents and the like. You don't want to "short-change" other shareholders who have put up cash or tangible property of determinative value.

Here are some examples of stock issuance scenarios for a small corporation (also see the sidebar "How to Authorize the Issuance of Shares"):

Issuance of Shares for Cash: If a shareholder will pay cash for her shares, simply type "Cash" for the consideration, and the dollar amount of the cash payment as the fair value of the payment. For example:

NAME	NUMBER OF SHARES	CONSIDERATION	FAIR VALUE
Richard Hoorn	100	Cash	$10,000

Issuance of Shares for Specific Items of Property: If a shareholder will purchase shares by transferring property to the corporation—we are referring to specific items of property here, such as a computer system, a truck or a patent—be as specific as you can when entering the consideration (for example, "1987 Ford pickup, vehicle ID #_____") and show the fair market value of the property (in the case of a vehicle, median blue book value is a good measure). For example:

NAME	NUMBER OF SHARES	CONSIDERATION	FAIR VALUE
Carol Sell	50	1987 Ford pickup (veh. # V1134R8976)	$5,000

Issuance of Shares for Assets of a Prior Business: If you are incorporating a prior unincorporated business, such as a sole proprietorship or partnership, and if an owner will transfer his part or full interest in it to the new corporation in return for shares, in the consideration column describe the prior business interest that will be transferred by each owner. Then add the fair market value of the business interest to the fair value column. For example:

NAME	NUMBER OF SHARES	CONSIDERATION	FAIR VALUE
Frank Laza	1,000	One-half interest in the assets of the partnership 'Just Partners,' as more fully described in a Bill of Sale to be prepared and attached to these Minutes	$100,000
Harry Hunt	1,000	One-half interest in the assets of the partnership 'Just Partners,' as more fully described in a Bill of Sale to be prepared and attached to these Minutes	$100,000

The Bill of Sale mentioned above can be prepared as explained in Chapter 6, Section C3.

Issuance of Shares for Cancellation of Indebtedness: If shares will be issued for the cancellation of indebtedness owed by the corporation to a shareholder, a description of the debt should be given as the consideration for the shares—for example: "cancellation of a promissory note dated May 15, 2000." In the fair value column, you should insert the dollar amount of the remaining unpaid principal amount due on the debt plus any accrued and unpaid interest. A copy of the note or other written evidence of the debt should be attached to the Minutes. This type of stock issuance isn't typical, since a newly formed corporation will not normally owe shareholders any amounts except, perhaps, by way of small advances made to help meet organizational costs, which will be reimbursed by the corporation directly.

Issuance of Shares for Past Services: If you will be issuing shares to a shareholder in return for past services actually rendered to the corporation, in the consideration column indicate the date and name of the person who provided the services—for example, "Services rendered the corporation by Betty Boop on January 5 to February 15, 2010." In the fair value column, put the fair market value of the services performed by the shareholder. A bill, or invoice, from the shareholder to the corporation showing the amount due for these services should be attached to your Minutes. Remember, you cannot issue shares for services that have yet to be performed.

⑰ Signature of Secretary: The corporate Secretary signs on the last page of the Minutes *after* the board approves the Minutes, as explained in Section B below.

B. Hold the First Meeting of the Board of Directors

As mentioned above, after preparing your Minutes, we suggest you actually hold a meeting with all your

directors present. Although only a quorum is required to attend, we think it is sensible to have as many directors present as possible. Each director should review and agree to the resolutions contained in your Minutes. As a reminder, make sure to do the following after the end of the meeting:

1. Date, and have each director sign, the Waiver of Notice form (the first page of the Minutes).
2. Indicate which directors were present and absent by checking the appropriate box to the right of each director's name on the title page of the Minutes.
3. Have the corporate Secretary sign the last page of the Minutes.

C. Consolidate Your Papers

After completing and approving the Minutes, do the following:

- Have your Secretary sign, date and seal (if desired) the "Certificate" section at the end of the Bylaws you prepared in Chapter 4.
- Place your Minutes and all attachments (copies of your Articles stamped by the California Secretary of State, Bylaws certified by your corporate Secretary, a sample stock certificate, any copies of notes cancelled, bills for services rendered, bills of sale and balance sheet for a prior unincorporated business) in your corporate records binder.
- Keep your corporate records binder at the corporation's principal executive office. An important part of corporate life is keeping your records properly, so be sure to document future corporate transactions—by preparing standard minutes of annual director and shareholder meetings—and place copies of corporate minutes and other documents in your corporate records.

TO PREPARE ONGOING CORPORATE MINUTES

The Corporate Minutes Book, The Legal Guide to Taking Care of Corporate Business, by Anthony Mancuso (Nolo Press), shows you how to prepare standard minutes of annual and special director and shareholder meetings for an existing corporation. It also contains resolutions to approve the various legal, tax, financial and business transactions that commonly occur during the life of a small corporation. All forms and resolutions are provided as tear-outs and forms on disk.

CONGRATULATIONS!

You have now completed the Minutes of your first board of directors meeting. We explain how to accomplish your last major organizational task, issuing your shares, in Chapter 6. Stay with us, you're just one step away from completing your incorporation.

■

CHAPTER 6

Issue Shares of Stock

The next and final incorporation step is issuing the shares of your corporation to your initial shareholders. Issuing shares is important not only to formally divide up ownership and voting interests in your corporation, but also to fulfill one of the substantial formalities required in your incorporation process. As a general rule, you should not begin doing business as a corporation until you have completed this step. That's because, as we discussed in Chapter 1, Section A3, you must *act* like a corporation to qualify for the legal protections and tax advantages the corporate form offers. To be sure you and your co-founders are protected by the limited liability that corporations provide, issue your shares as soon as possible, before conducting any business under your corporate name.

Your initial issuance of shares (as well as any subsequent issuances) must be accomplished in accordance with California and federal securities laws. For the purposes of this book, this means complying with the rules of the California limited offering exemption—the main private offering exemption we discussed in the text of Chapter 1, Section C1. (As we explained in Chapter 1, generally corporations that qualify for the California limited offering exemption will also qualify for the federal private offering exemption). There are two formalities associated with this exemption that you should attend to before issuing shares of stock—you must prepare a "representation letter" for each shareholder and a "Notice of Stock Transaction" form to be filed with the Secretary of State. Preparing these forms will be simple since you've already recorded the necessary information (the initial shareholders, the amounts of shares they'll buy and how they'll pay for them) in your stock issuance resolution in the Minutes of the First Board Meeting (that you prepared as explained in the previous Chapter). We look at these forms in Sections A and B below, then get to the actual issuance of shares in Section C.

A. Prepare Shareholder Representation Letters

This section shows you how to prepare shareholder representation letters, which document your compliance with the California limited offering exemption. Before preparing these letters, make sure to do the following:

- Re-read Chapter 1, Section C1, to be sure your initial stock issuance qualifies for the California limited offering exemption. If you have any doubts, consult a lawyer.
- Be sure that you have disclosed all facts concerning the finances and business of the corporation, as well as the terms and conditions of your proposed stock issuance, to all prospective shareholders. You should provide this disclosure in writing and be able to prove that full disclosure was made to all shareholders—remember, state and federal securities laws require you to disclose all material facts.

You need to prepare a shareholder representation letter for *each* of your initial shareholders (this includes each person, such as a spouse, who will jointly own shares in your corporation). So, to start this step, make a photocopy of the shareholder representation letter contained in the Appendix of this book for each of your prospective shareholders. Below is a sample of the shareholder representation letter. Complete a separate letter for each person who will be an initial shareholder in your corporation according to the sample form and instructions on the next page.

- ✔ The parenthetical blanks, i.e., " _(information)_ ," indicate information that you must complete on the form.
- ✔ Each circled number (e.g., ❶) refers to a special instruction that provides specific information to help you complete an item. The special instructions immediately follow the sample form.
- ✔ Fill in the tear-out form using a typewriter or printer with a black-ink ribbon.

CALIFORNIA LIMITED OFFERING EXEMPTION REVIEW

Let's look at the most important reasons for preparing a representation letter for each prospective shareholder when relying on the California limited offering exemption.

- The California limited offering exemption requires each purchaser of shares to represent that she is purchasing the shares for her own investment and not for resale.
- Each purchaser of California limited offering shares should document in writing the fact that she fits within one of the shareholder suitability categories discussed in Chapter 1, Section C1.
- If a purchaser relying on the limited offering exemption does not fit within one of the suitability categories (she is not a director, officer or promoter of the corporation, does not have a pre-existing relation to or relationship with any of these corporate people, and does not have qualifying financial or investment qualifications), she should designate, in writing, a professional advisor who has sufficient business or financial experience to protect her interests.
- Qualifying for this exemption can be made more certain by documenting the fact that the shareholders have received a full disclosure of all material facts and have had an opportunity to ask questions and receive answers concerning the terms and conditions of the stock issuance. The shareholder representation letter we include documents these important representations.

SHAREHOLDER REPRESENTATION LETTER

To:

_____ *(name of corporation)* _____
_____ *(address)* _____
_____ *(city, state, zip)* _____ ❶

I, ___ *(name of shareholder)* ___, ❷ in connection with my purchase of ___ *(number of shares)* ___ ❷ common shares of the corporation named above, hereby make the following representations:

A. I am a suitable purchaser of these shares under the California limited offering exemption because:

(Check the box to the left of one of the following clauses that describes how you qualify as a suitable purchaser of shares under the California limited offering exemption.) ❸

1. [ ] I am a director, officer or promoter of the corporation, or I occupy a position with the corporation with duties and authority substantially similar to those of an executive officer of the corporation.

2. [ ] I have a pre-existing personal and/or business relationship with the corporation, or one or more of its directors, officers or controlling persons, consisting of personal or business contacts of a nature and duration that enables me to be aware of the character, business acumen and general business and financial circumstances of the person (including the corporation) with whom such relationship exists.

3. [ ] I have the capacity to protect my own interests in connection with my purchase of the above shares by reason of my own business and/or financial experience.

(Check box 4(a) or box 4(b) below if it applies; check both boxes if they both apply.)

4(a).[ ] Pursuant to Section 260.102.13(e) of Title 10 of the California Code of Regulations, I am purchasing $150,000 or more of the corporation's shares, and either 1) my investment (including mandatory assessments) does not exceed 10% of my net worth or joint net worth with my spouse, or 2) by reason of my own business and/or financial experience, or the business and/or financial experience of my professional advisor (who is unaffiliated with and not compensated by the corporation or any of its affiliates or selling agents), I have, or my professional advisor has, the capacity to protect my own interests in connection with the purchase of these shares.

4(b). [ ] Pursuant to Section 260.102.13(g) of Title 10 of the California Code of Regulations, I am an "accredited investor" under Rule 501(a) of Regulation D adopted by the Securities and Exchange Commission under the Securities Act of 1933. This means either 1) my individual net worth, or joint net worth with my spouse, at the time of the purchase of these shares, exceeds $ 1,000,000; 2) my individual income is in excess of $200,000 in each of the two most recent years or my joint income with my spouse is in excess of $300,000 in each of those years, and I have a reasonable expectation of reaching the same income level in the current year; or 3) I qualify under one of the other accredited investor categories of Rule 501(a) of SEC Regulation D.

(Check box 5(a) if it applies. If so, provide information in 5(a) and 5(b)(1) and 5(b)(2), and have professional advisor date and sign under 5(b)(3) below.)

5(a). [ ] I have the capacity to protect my own interests in connection with my purchase of the above shares by reason of the business and/or financial experience of __*(name of professional advisor)*__, whom I have engaged and hereby designate as my professional advisor in connection with my purchase of the above shares.

5(b). __*(Name of professional advisor)*__ hereby represents:

(1) I have been engaged as the professional advisor of __*(name of shareholder)*__ and have provided him or her with investment advice in connection with the purchase of __*(number of shares)*__ common shares in __*(name of corporation)*__.

(2) As a regular part of my business as a/an __*(profession)*__, I am customarily relied upon by others for investment recommendations or decisions and I am customarily compensated for such services, either specifically or by way of compensation for related professional services.

(3) I am unaffiliated with and am not compensated by the corporation or any affiliate or selling agent of the corporation, directly or indirectly. I do not have, nor will I have (a) a relationship of employment with the corporation, either as an employee, employer, independent contractor or principal; (b) the beneficial ownership of securities of the corporation,

its affiliates or selling agents, in excess of 1% of its securities; or (c) a relationship with the corporation such that I control, am controlled by, or am under common control with the corporation, and, more specifically, a relationship by which I possess, directly or indirectly, the power to direct, or cause the direction, of the management, policies or actions of the corporation.

Dated: *(date of signing)*

   (signature of professional advisor)
(type name of advisor)

6. [ ] I am the spouse, relative, or relative of the spouse of another suitable purchaser of shares, and I have the same principal residence as this purchaser.

B. I represent that I am purchasing these shares for investment for my own account and not with a view to, or for, sale in connection with any distribution of the shares. I understand that these shares have not been qualified or registered under any state or federal securities law and that they may not be transferred or otherwise disposed of without such qualification or registration pursuant to such laws or an opinion of legal counsel satisfactory to the corporation that such qualification or registration is not required.

C. I have not received any advertisement or general solicitation with respect to the sale of the shares of the above named corporation.

D. I represent that, before signing this document, I have been provided access to, or been given, all material facts relevant to the purchase of my shares, including all financial and written information about the corporation and the terms and conditions of the stock offering and that I have been given the opportunity to ask questions and receive answers concerning any additional terms and conditions of the stock offering or other information which I, or my professional advisor if I have designated one, felt necessary to protect my interests in connection with the stock purchase transaction.❹

Dated: *(date of signing)* ❺

   (signature of shareholder)   ❺
(type name of shareholder)

Special Instructions

❶ Insert the name of your corporation and street address of the principal office of the corporation.

❷ Insert into the first blank the name of the shareholder for whom the letter is being prepared. In the second blank in this paragraph, indicate the number of shares being purchased by the shareholder (for joint owners, insert the *full* number of shares being purchased jointly in the each shareholder letter). For example, if John and Mary Butterworth will purchase 100 shares jointly, prepare one letter for John's purchase of an interest in 100 shares, and a second letter for Mary's purchase of these same 100 shares (you do not have to specify that each is taking one half of the joint interest—the letter is concerned with each person's *qualification as a purchaser* under the limited offering exemption, not with the amount of shares each will buy).

❸ Complete Section A of the letter by checking *at least one box* to show how the shareholder qualifies as a suitable purchaser of shares under the California limited offering exemption. Checking more than one box is perfectly OK—doing so simply means a shareholder qualifies in more than one way as a suitable purchaser of shares. For simplicity, related suitability categories have been grouped under a single checkbox. Here is the breakdown of how each checkbox paragraph under Section A of this letter matches up with the suitability categories discussed in Chapter 1, Section C1:

Paragraph A Checkbox	Limited Offering Suitability Category
1	Director or Officer of the Corporation, Executive Officer of the Corporation, or Promoter of the Corporation
2	Individual With a Pre-existing Personal or Business Relationship With the Corporation or any of its Officers, Directors or Controlling Persons
3	Sophisticated Investor
4(a)	Major Investor
4(b)	Accredited Investor
5	Investor With Professional Advisor
6	Relative of Another Suitable Shareholder

For example, if you are preparing a letter for a director or officer of your corporation, check box A1 to show that the shareholder fits within the exemption as a director of your corporation. If you are preparing a letter for a spouse of one of these directors or officers (and the spouse shares the same principal residence as the director or officer), check the box next to A6 to show that this shareholder is suitable under the limited offering exemption as a relative of another suitable shareholder. If a shareholder qualifies because he is relying on the financial or business experience of a professional advisor to protect his interests in the stock purchase transaction, check box 5(a) and indicate the name of the professional advisor on the blank line in this paragraph (see the sidebar, "Who Can Be a Professional Advisor?"). Then complete all the blanks in Section 5(b)(1) and (2) and have your professional advisor sign and date the advisor representation at the bottom of Section 5(b)(3). Type the advisor's name directly under her signature line. (Or in case the shareholder is relying on the Major Investor category and has a professional advisor, check 4(a) and complete 5(b) as explained just above).

❹ Paragraphs B, C and D of each shareholder letter contain representations important for qualifying under the California limited offering exemption as explained in Chapter 1, Section C1. By signing the letter, each shareholder agrees that these representations are true. Make sure each shareholder reads these paragraphs and understands their effect before she signs the letter.

USE A STOCK CERTIFICATE LEGEND TO REMIND SHAREHOLDERS OF TRANSFER LIMITATIONS

The tear-out stock certificates in the Appendix of this book contain a legend that alerts your shareholders to the representations and restrictions contained in paragraph B of the shareholder letter. Adding this legend to stock certificates is not a legal requirement of the California limited offering exemption, but we think it makes sense to add one just to remind your shareholders that shares cannot be freely transferred without complying with state and federal securities laws (this legend also helps you qualify your stock issuance under the federal private offering exemption as discussed in Chapter 1, section C2). If you order pre-printed stock certificates, you may wish to type this legend on the face of your printed certificates. If so, simply copy the language that appears in bold capital letters on the face of this book's tear-out certificates. (In addition, most legal stationers will print a legend with the same or similar language on specially ordered certificates for an additional charge.)

❺ Have each shareholder sign and date her representation letter. Remember, if you check box 5(a)—or sometimes 4(a)—for any shareholder, make sure the shareholder has her professional advisor date and sign under paragraph 5(b)(3) of the letter. Make a copy of each completed shareholder representation letter to place in your corporate records binder, and give each shareholder the completed original.

WHO CAN BE A PROFESSIONAL ADVISOR?

Attorneys, certified public accountants (CPAs), persons licensed or registered as broker-dealers, agents or investment advisors, and banks and savings and loan associations are qualified to act as professional advisors. This list is not exhaustive, however, and you may also rely on and designate a person as a professional advisor "who, as a regular part of such person's business, is customarily relied upon by others for investment recommendations or decisions, and who is customarily compensated for such services, either specifically or by way of compensation for related professional services."

Professional advisors must be "unaffiliated" with, and not be directly or indirectly compensated by, the corporation or by any of the corporation's affiliates or selling agents.

B. Prepare and File Notice of Stock Transaction Form

When issuing your initial shares under the California limited offering exemption, you must prepare and file a "Notice of Transaction Pursuant to Corporations Code Section 25102(f)" with the California Department of Corporations. (This department is not under the Secretary of State—it is a different state agency that regulates the sale of securities.) This notice informs the Department of Corporations that your corporation is relying on the Section 25102(f) limited offering exemption, so that you can issue your shares without following the regulations required for large public offerings. This form must be filed with the Department of Corporations within 15 calendar days after the first sale of shares. Your first sale of shares generally occurs the first time your corporation receives payment from any shareholder for any of your initial shares (but see the note "Technically, When

Does the First Sale of Shares Occur?" below). If you follow the sequence contained in this chapter, you will receive all of the payments for your shares when you actually issue them in the next section (Section C below, "Issue Shares of Stock"). However, we suggest you prepare and file the Notice of Stock Transaction form now, before you sell your shares. By doing this, you'll be more likely to mail your notice form to the Department of Corporations on time.

 TECHNICALLY, WHEN DOES THE FIRST SALE OF SHARES OCCUR?

Legally, the first sale occurs when the corporation has obtained a contractual commitment from a shareholder to purchase one or more of the shares it intends to sell. Since we assume that you have not entered into a formal pre-issuance commitment, such as a shareholder's subscription agreement, where a shareholder promises to buy a certain number of shares in the future for a stated price, the first sale occurs when the corporation receives the first pay-ment for shares. (If you do ask one or more share-holders to sign an agreement of this sort, you must file the notice form within 15 days after the signing of the first of these agreements.)

 WHAT IF YOU FILE THE NOTICE LATE?

A failure to file this notice form within the time limit will not result in your loss of the ability to rely on this exemption. However, if you don't file the notice on time, the Department may issue a demand for the notice, and then you must file the notice form within 15 business days after the demand, and pay the fees that would have been due if you issued your shares under a normal permit procedure (a much more costly process). In addition, a late filing is a violation of the California securities laws and may subject you to other penalties. Our conclusion: Keep things simple and file this notice form before the specified deadline.

BEFORE YOU PREPARE AND FILE THE STOCK ISSUANCE NOTICE FORM, DO THE FOLLOWING:

Make sure you are certain of all of the details of your initial stock issuance (for instance, who will purchase your shares and the type and amount of payment to be received for the shares). Of course, at this stage in your incorpo-ration, this should be no problem, as the details of your stock issuance should be contained in the stock issuance resolution of your Minutes, prepared as explained in Chapter 5.

Include ALL shares being sold under your initial issuance. No subsequent notices need to be filed with the state for sales of shares in connection with the same "transaction"—your initial issuance. But remember, you will need to obtain a permit or seek another exemption for any subsequent issuances of shares.

If you decide to file a federal notice form with the federal Securities and Exchange Commission under one of the rules of Regulation D—to ensure that your issuance qualifies for a federal exemption (see Chapter 1, Section C2)—you can dispense with the notice form shown here and send the California Department of Corporations a copy of your federal Notice D form instead, together with a cover letter and the proper filing fee (see Section 260.102.14 of Title 10 of the California Code of Regulations for further information). We don't expect most small closely held corporations to make this federal Regulation D filing, and we therefore assume that you will have to file the California notice form discussed in this section.

WHAT IF YOU SELL YOUR SHARES TO OUT-OF-STATE SHAREHOLDERS?

This California notice form is not required if none of your shares are purchased in California. We assume, however, that all or most of your shares will be purchased in this state by California residents. *If you sell shares out-of-state, you must comply with the state securities laws and procedures of the other states.*

1. Prepare the Notice Form

A "Notice of Transaction Pursuant to Corporations Code Section 25102(f)" is included in the Appendix of this book. Fill out the Notice form according to the sample form and instructions below.

✔ The parenthetical blanks, i.e., " _(information)_ ," indicate information that you must complete on the form.

✔ Each circled number (e.g., ❶) refers to a special instruction that provides specific information to help you complete an item. The special instructions immediately follow the sample form.

✔ Fill in the tear-out form using a typewriter or printer with a black-ink ribbon.

 MAKE SURE TO USE THE LATEST VERSION OF THE NOTICE FORM

The Appendix contains the most recent version of this form as of the date of this printing of the book—currently form version 10/84. The official number of this form is 260.102.14(c). As forms occasionally change, you may want to call the Department of Corporations to be sure the 10/84 version of the notice form is current at the time of your stock issuance (or is still being accepted for filing if it has been superseded). To do this, call one of the offices of the Department of Corporations listed below. If they are not accepting this version of the form, ask the clerk to send you one or two copies of the most recent Notice form.

Department of Corporations Telephone Numbers

Los Angeles	213-736-2741
Sacramento	916-445-7205
San Diego	619-525-4233
San Francisco	415-557-3787

SAMPLE NOTICE OF STOCK TRANSACTION FORM

(Department of Corporations Use Only)   Department of Corporations File No., if any

Fee Paid $ _____

Receipt No. _____   _____
(Insert File Number(s) of Previous Filings
Before the Department, if any) ❶

FEE: $25.00 $35.00 $50.00 $150.00 $300.00
(Circle the appropriate amount of fee.
See Corp. Code Section 25608(c)) ❷

COMMISSIONER OF CORPORATIONS
STATE OF CALIFORNIA

NOTICE OF TRANSACTION PURSUANT TO CORPORATIONS CODE SECTION 25102(f)

A. Check one: Transaction under [**X**] ❸ Section 25102(f)   [ ] Rule 260.103.
❹

1. Name of Issuer: _____

2. Address of Issuer: _____
                           Street   City   State   ZIP

   Mailing Address: _____
                           Street   City   State   ZIP

3. Area Code and Telephone Number: _____

4. Issuer's state (or other jurisdiction) of incorporation or organization: _____

_____

5. Title of class or classes of securities sold in transaction: _____

_____

6. The value of the securities sold or proposed to be sold in the transaction, determined
in accordance with Corp. Code Section 25608(g) in connection with the fee required upon
filing this notice, is (fee based on amount shown in line (iii) under "Total Offering"):

	California	Total Offering
(a) (i) in mone	$_____	$_____
(ii) in consideration other than money	$_____	$_____
(iii) total of (i) and (ii)	$_____	$_____

(b)   ( ) Change in rights, preferences, privileges or restrictions of or
          on outstanding securities. ($25.00 fee)   (See Rule 260.103)

7. Type of filing under Securities Act of 1933, if applicable: _____

_____

8. Date of Notice: _____   _____
                                                          Issuer
( ) Check if issuer already has a   _____
    consent to service of process
    on file with the Commissioner.   Authorized Signature on behalf of issuer

                                        _____
                                        Print name and title of signatory
Name, Address and Phone number of contact person:

_____

_____

_____

Instruction: Each issuer (other than a California corporation) filing a notice under Section
25102(f) must file a consent to service of process (Form 260.165), unless it already has a consent to service on file with the Commissioner.
260.102.14(c) (10/84)

Special Instructions

❶ **Top of Form:** Ignore the lines at the upper left and right portions of the form; the lines at the upper left will be filled out by the Department of Corporations, and the line at the upper right is only for corporations that have previously qualified securities with the Department and have been issued a Department File Number.

❷ **Fee Heading: Do not circle a fee.** The state of California has suspended fees for filing this form until June 2000. Until then, filing this form is free.

❸ **Item A:** Check the box titled "Section 25102(f)" so that this line reads "Transaction under (X) Section 25102(f)"—this means that the form is being used to provide notice of your stock issuance under the California limited offering exemption.

❹ Now let's look at each of the numbered lines in the remainder of the notice form:

- 1. Type the name of your corporation exactly as it appears in your Articles of Incorporation.
- 2. Type the principal address of the corporation—provide a full street address (not a P.O. Box), including the city, state and zip code. If you use a separate mailing address for your corporation, show it on the second line.
- 3. Type the telephone number of the corporation, including the area code.
- 4. Type "California" on this line to indicate California as the state of your incorporation.
- 5. Type "Common Stock" in this blank to indicate that you are issuing only one class of common shares. Of course, we assume that you have formed your corporation by filing the Articles of Incorporation included with this book (prepared as explained in Chapter 3), which provide for one class of common shares only.
- 6(a). In these blanks, show the value of the shares that you will sell to your shareholders. For most small closely held corporations, the value of the corporation's initial shares is the same as the payments you recorded in the stock issuance resolution contained in the Minutes of the First Board Meeting (prepared as explained in Chapter 5). (But

see the sidebar "Valuing Shares to Be Issued for Property and Past Services" below.) Simply add up all cash and noncash dollar amounts from the Fair Value column of the stock issuance resolution in your Minutes, then place these totals in the blanks here.

VALUING SHARES TO BE ISSUED FOR PROPERTY AND PAST SERVICES

The legal rule that will apply to most, if not all, privately held corporations is that the value of your shares is:

(1) the actual price to be paid for the shares (if the shares are purchased for cash) or

(2) the actual (fair market) value of any noncash consideration, such as property or the performance of completed services) to be received for the shares.

However, in the unlikely (but theoretically possible) event that the value of your shares when issued is greater than the cash price or actual value of any noncash payment made for the shares, then this higher figure should be used when filling in these blanks on the Notice form. This might be the case if there are outside market pressures driving up share values or outside investors vying for your initial shares, but generally, your initial shares should only be worth the cash amount or actual value of the property or services paid for them by your initial shareholders.

Here's how to fill in each of the blanks in line 6(a) of the notice form:

1) Indicate the total amount of all cash payments to be made by your California shareholders in the California column of blank 6(a)(i).
2) Indicate the total value of all noncash payments to be made by your California shareholders in the California column of blank 6(a)(ii).
3) Total the above amounts and place the result in the California column of blank 6(a)(iii).
4) If all initial shareholders will be California shareholders, carry over the three California amounts to

the corresponding row of the "Total Offering" column in Item 6(a). If you will sell shares outside of California, add the out-of-state cash and non-cash figures to the California figures and place these totals in the corresponding rows in the "Total Offering" column. Then provide a new overall total in the Total Offering column of blank 6(a)(iii). Remember: if you sell shares out-of-state, you also must comply with the other states' securities laws.

The calculations here are really quite easy and are best demonstrated with an example or two.

Example 1: *You plan to issue a total of 30,000 initial shares for cash and property totaling $30,000: $10,000 in cash; $20,000 as the fair market value of all the property to be transferred for shares. All your prospective shareholders are California residents. You fill out Item 6(a) in the Notice form as follows:*

	California	Total Offering
(a) (i) in money	$ 10,000	$ 10,000
(ii) in consideration other than money	$ 20,000	$ 20,000
(iii) total of (i) and (ii)	$ 30,000	$ 30,000

Example 2: *Assume the same facts as the previous example except that 5,000 shares will also be issued to an out-of-state shareholder in return for $5,000 cash. In this case, the Total Offering column figures will be changed to reflect this out-of-state amount as follows:*

	California	Total Offering
(a) (i) in money	$ 10,000	$ 15,000
(ii) in consideration other than money	$ 20,000	$ 20,000
(iii) total of (i) and (ii)	$ 30,000	$ 35,000

- 6(b). Ignore this box, which reads "Change in rights, preferences, privileges or restrictions of or on outstanding securities." It applies to transactions other than the type we are talking about here.
- 7. In answer to the "Type of filing under Securities Act of 1933, if applicable," type "None." This question relates to the federal securities laws.

  If you are actually registering your stock offering or filing a notice with the SEC (with the help of a lawyer), the attorney who is helping you with your federal filing will indicate "Registered" in the blank or show the number of the exemption under which the federal filing was made (such as one of the federal Regulation D exemption rules—see Chapter 1, Section C2).

- 8. Skip "Date of Notice" for a moment. To the right, above the word "Issuer," type the name of the corporation. Skip the line labeled "Authorized Signature on behalf of issuer" for a moment. On the line below, marked "Print name and title of signatory," type the name of a corporate officer or director who will sign this Notice form and then, on the lines marked "Name, Address and Phone Number of Contact Person," type this person's name, address and phone number. (The contact person is the person the Department will notify in the event there are any questions concerning the Notice form.) Then have this person date and sign the form on the lines marked "Date of Notice" and "Authorized Signature on behalf of issuer." Make sure to have this person date and sign two additional copies of the Notice as well (you will mail two copies for filing with the Department of Corporations as explained below, and keep the original for your records).

Ignore the printed parenthetical blank "( )" under Item 8, which reads "Check if issuer already has a consent to service of process on file with the Commissioner." As the official instructions at the bottom of the form indicate, California corporations do not need to file a consent to service of process.

2. File the Notice Form

Make sure your two copies of your prepared Notice are dated and signed as explained in the instructions to line 8 in the preceding section. To the file notice, mail the two dated and signed copies, together with a stamped, self-addressed envelope (self-addressed to the person who signed your Notice form, c/o your corporation) to:

Department of Corporations
980 9th Street, Suite 500
Sacramento, CA 95814

You can also file the notice in person at any branch office of the Department of Corporations (Los Angeles, San Francisco or San Diego). However, most incorporators will find mailing the notice to the main Sacramento office the most convenient means of making this filing. Within a week or so after mailing, you should receive a copy of your Notice in the return envelope, file-stamped by the Department. Place this copy in your corporate records binder.

C. Issue Shares of Stock

The final step in your incorporation process is issuing the initial shares of your corporation to your shareholders. Ten blank, ready-to-use stock certificates are included in the Appendix at the back of this book. If you want to order specially printed certificates for your corporation, you can do so by ordering one of the corporate kits offered by Nolo Press (see the order form at the back of the book).

1. Prepare and Distribute Stock Certificates

Fill in the blanks on the tear-out stock certificates contained in the Appendix at the back of the book (or on the specially printed certificates you have ordered) as you follow the special instructions and sample below. You should fill out one stock certificate for each shareholder or each pair of joint shareholders (for example, spouses who own shares as community property). Each stock certificate should represent the number of shares the corporation is issuing to a particular shareholder (or pair of joint shareholders).

A FEW REMINDERS BEFORE YOU ISSUE YOUR INITIAL SHARES

- All of your initial shares should be sold for the same price per share. (When you prepared the Minutes of the First Board Meeting, you should have decided on the price per share for your initial shares—see Chapter 5, Section A.)
- Your corporation cannot issue more shares than the number of shares authorized by your Articles of Incorporation. (As we've said, it's common for corporations to authorize more shares in their Articles than they will actually issue here.)
- Of course, by now you know that to use the procedure in this book, you must issue your initial shares under the California limited offering exemption. See Chapter 1, Section C1, to refresh yourself on these rules.

IF YOU ARE YOU INCORPORATING A PRIOR BUSINESS, YOU MAY NEED TO COMPLY WITH CALIFORNIA'S BULK SALES LAW FORMALITIES

A few special pre-stock issuance formalities apply to some readers who are incorporating a pre-existing business: making one or more publications and filings to comply with California's Bulk Sales Law (under Division 6 of the California Commercial Code, starting with Section 6101). Generally, this law applies to you if:

- You are transferring more than half the value of the inventory and equipment of an unincorporated California business to your new corporation. (In other words, you are incorporating an existing sole proprietorship or partnership); and
- The value of the business assets being transferred is $10,000 or more; and
- The business being incorporated is engaged in the principal business of selling inventory from stock (such as a retail or wholesale business, including a business that manufactures what it sells) or is a restaurant.

The purpose of this law is to prevent business owners from secretly transferring the "bulk" of the assets of their business to another entity in an attempt to avoid paying creditors and to prevent schemes whereby the prior business owners "sell out" (usually to a relative at bargain prices) and come back into the business through a back door later on. Of course, we know that you intend no such thing, and that, if this law applies to you, it is simply because you are incorporating a prior business (and that your corporation will gladly assume and pay off any debts still owed by the prior unincorporated business).

If all three above conditions do not apply to your incorporation of an unincorporated business, you can ignore this law.

If all three conditions do apply, what you must do to comply with the law depends on whether your new corporation will assume the debts of the prior, unincorporated business (and can remain solvent after the assumption of these debts). If your corporation does assume the debts (most do), you must publish and send a Notice of Bulk Sale and Assumption to all the creditors of the prior unincorporated business within 30 days of the transfer of assets (normally, the assets are transferred when shares are issued to the initial shareholders).

If your corporation will not assume the debts of the prior business, you must publish a Notice of Bulk Sale at least 12 days *before* the transfer takes place.

A local legal newspaper can make the required publication and filing for you for a small fee (and will provide the necessary forms). The publication and filing must be made in the county where the unincorporated business was located.

Example: *Five people incorporate their online design business and the corporation issues shares to them. The price of all of the shares to be initially issued is established at $50 per share. For their shares, Jack pays $10,000, Sam $5,000, Julie $2,500 and Sid and Nancy (a married couple) give the corporation a computer with a fair market value of $1,000. Jack receives Stock Certificate # 1 for 200 shares, Sam receives Certificate # 2 for 100 shares, Julie Certificate # 3 for 50 shares and Sid and Nancy Certificate #4 for 20 shares.*

The appropriate information should also be completed on the stock certificate stubs. The stubs in the Appendix and from Nolo Press's Records Kit are perforated to tear away from each certificate, but in the Portfolio Corporate Records Kits, the stubs are contained on separate stub pages—these pages, and the information recorded on them, stay in your corporate records binder.

✔ The parenthetical blanks, i.e., " _(information)_ ," indicate information that you must complete on the form.

✔ Each circled number (e.g., ❶) refers to a special instruction that provides specific information to help you complete an item. The special instructions immediately follow the sample form.

✔ Fill in the tear-out certificates using a typewriter or printer with a black-ink ribbon.

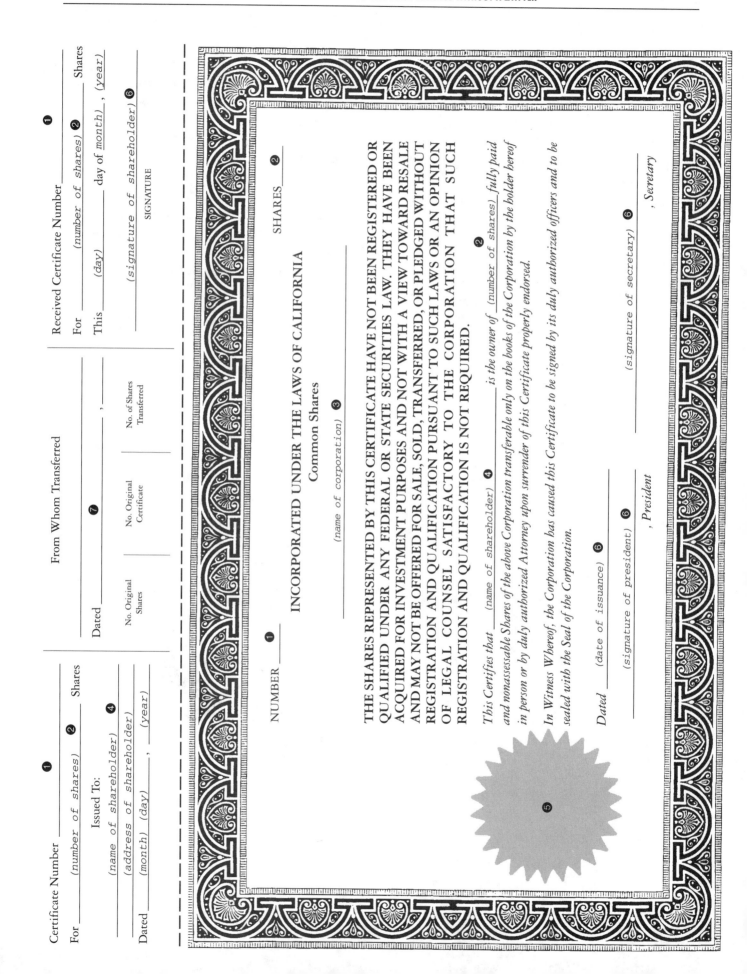

Certificate Number _____ ❶

For _____ ❷ Shares
        (number of shares)

Issued To:

_____ ❹
(name of shareholder)

_____
(address of shareholder)

Dated _____ , _____ , _____
       (month)   (day)   (year)

From Whom Transferred

Dated _____ , _____

No. Original Shares	No. Original Certificate	No. of Shares Transferred

❼

Certificate Number _____ ❶

Received Certificate Number _____

For _____ ❷ _____ Shares
        (number of shares)

This _____ day of _____ , _____
      (day)   month   (year)

_____ ❻
(signature of shareholder)

SIGNATURE

NUMBER _____ ❶   SHARES _____ ❷

INCORPORATED UNDER THE LAWS OF CALIFORNIA

Common Shares

_____ ❸
(name of corporation)

THE SHARES REPRESENTED BY THIS CERTIFICATE HAVE NOT BEEN REGISTERED OR QUALIFIED UNDER ANY FEDERAL OR STATE SECURITIES LAW. THEY HAVE BEEN ACQUIRED FOR INVESTMENT PURPOSES AND NOT WITH A VIEW TOWARD RESALE AND MAY NOT BE OFFERED FOR SALE, SOLD, TRANSFERRED, OR PLEDGED WITHOUT REGISTRATION AND QUALIFICATION PURSUANT TO SUCH LAWS OR AN OPINION OF LEGAL COUNSEL SATISFACTORY TO THE CORPORATION THAT SUCH REGISTRATION AND QUALIFICATION IS NOT REQUIRED.

This Certifies that _____ ❹ _____ is the owner of _____ ❷ _____ fully paid
                    (name of shareholder)   (number of shares)
and nonassessable Shares of the above Corporation transferable only on the books of the Corporation by the holder hereof in person or by duly authorized Attorney upon surrender of this Certificate properly endorsed.

In Witness Whereof, the Corporation has caused this Certificate to be signed by its duly authorized officers and to be sealed with the Seal of the Corporation.

Dated _____ ❻
        (date of issuance)

❺

_____ ❻
(signature of president)

, President

_____ ❻
(signature of secretary)

, Secretary

HOW WILL SPOUSES TAKE TITLE TO STOCK?

There are a few common ways in which spouses take title to shares:

Sole Ownership. Often a married person will take title to stock in his or her name alone. This is perfectly legal, even if community property (money or property purchased with money earned by either spouse during a marriage) is used to buy the shares. The other (non-listed) spouse has a half interest in the stock even if his name doesn't appear on the stock certificate ownership line, and he can enforce his right to this interest if necessary (upon divorce or the death of the listed spouse).

Joint Tenancy. This form of ownership is often used by spouses wishing to co-own property, since, upon the death of one spouse (a joint tenant), the surviving spouse takes full title to the shares without the necessity of the property going through probate. Although joint tenancy shares cannot be willed to a third party, they can be sold or transferred during the life of a spouse (such a sale terminates the joint tenancy and turns the joint tenancy into tenancy in common—see below). Joint tenancy ownership is created by using the word "as joint tenants," or "in joint tenancy," on the ownership line (for example, "Michael Sullivan and Sally Sullivan, as joint tenants"). It is also common, but not legally necessary in California, to add the words "with right of survivorship" (for example, "Michael Sullivan and Sally Sullivan, as joint tenants with right of survivorship").

Community Property. Community property ownership can only be used by a husband and wife. Although spouses can use another joint ownership form, such as joint tenancy, community property ownership is often preferred when the stock is in fact purchased with community property. The reason is that, upon the death of a spouse, the property left by her is given a "stepped-up" basis equal to its value at the time of her death. If the property was held jointly as community property, both spouses' half-interests (the deceased and the surviving spouse's interests) will be given this stepped-up basis. (The normal rule—for joint tenancies—is that only the deceased spouse's half-interest in the property is given this increased basis.) This additional increase in basis will result in increased tax savings when the property is later sold or transferred.

Probate law has been simplified to the point where community property can generally be transferred easily and efficiently through probate to a surviving spouse. Note, however, that each spouse is free to leave their one-half share of community property to someone other than the spouse in a will; if a deceased spouse has done so, standard probate procedures will normally be required to transfer title to the non-spousal inheritor.

To show that shares are owned as the community property of spouses, simply take title by listing the spouses names, followed by the words, "as community property" (for example, "Michael Sullivan and Sally Sullivan, as community property").

Tenancy in Common. Spouses normally do not take title as tenants in common—this form of co-ownership is typically used by unrelated co-owners of shares. Each co-owner holds an equal interest in the property and can sell, transfer or will his or her interest to a third person at any time. Title to shares owned as a tenancy in common is shown by listing the co-owners' names, followed by the words "as tenants in common" (for example, "Reuben Ruiz and Herman Grizwold, as tenants in common").

Special Instructions

❶ Number the stock certificates on the certificate itself and the accompanying stub. Make sure to insert the number into all blanks labeled ❶. (But if you've ordered the Portfolio Corporate Records Kit, each stub page is already numbered.) You should number the stock certificates consecutively, and issue them in consecutive order. This is important, since it enables the corporation to keep track of who owns its shares.

❷ In the upper right-hand corner of the certificate, insert the number of shares that each certificate represents. (The number of shares each person is entitled to receive is indicated in the stock issuance resolution of your Minutes—see Chapter 5.) Also indicate this information on the stubs, in the blanks labeled ❷. Then add this information to the blank labeled ❷ lower on the certificate. Here you can simply put the number of shares represented by each stock certificate or spell it out—for example, "500" or "FIVE-HUN-DRED." Some incorporators prefer to do both—for example, "FIVE-HUNDRED (500)."

❸ Type the name of the corporation on the certificate exactly as it appears in your Articles of Incorporation.

❹ Type the name of the shareholder. If the stock certificate will be held by two persons, indicate both persons' names and the form of co-ownership here—for example, "Mai Chang and Lee Chang, as community property" or "Carolyn Kimura and Sally Silvestri, as joint tenants" (see sidebar "How Will Spouses Take Title to Stock?"). Also, on the stubs: type the shareholders' names and addresses, in the blanks labeled ❹.

❺ If you have ordered a corporate seal, an impression of the seal should be placed somewhere close to the bottom of each stock certificate. The impression of a seal on a stock certificate is not necessary—your certificates are legally valid with or without an impression of a corporate seal.

❻ The date of issuance on the stub and on the certificate, the shareholder signature line on the stub, and the president and secretary signature lines on the certificate will be filled out when you distribute your stock certificates as explained in Section C3 below.

❼ The transfer sections (on the stubs and on the back of each certificate) should be left blank for now. You will fill them in if and when the shares are later transferred by the original shareholders (when a shareholder retires, dies or just sells out). If you've ordered a corporate records kit, this also applies to the transfer sections on the stubs or the separate stub pages and on the back of each of the printed stock certificates.

After filling out the stock certificates and stubs, place the completed stubs in consecutive order in the stock certificate section of your corporate records binder. If you've ordered the Portfolio Corporate Records Kit, you do not need to detach or move the completed stub pages in the stock certificate section of the binder.

This book and the corporate kits contain a separate "Share Register" (and "Transfer Ledger"). Fill out one line of the Share Register for each shareholder (the Transfer Ledger is only used for future transfers of the original shares). Leave the date of issuance spaces blank until you distribute stock certificates as explained in Section C3 below. Instructions included with the Nolo Records Kit show you how to complete each section of the records binder, including these Share Register and Transfer Ledger pages.

2. Prepare Shareholder Receipts

After filling out your stock certificates, before you distribute them, you may wish to prepare receipts for your shareholders or, if incorporating a prior business, a bill of sale for the purchase of the prior business. You are not legally required to prepare these forms but we think it's generally good business to do so—and a sensible precaution to take to avoid later confusion as to who paid what for initial shares in your corporation.

A blank Bill of Sale and separate receipts are contained in the Appendix of this book. Here are the names of the various receipts for the different types of payments that can be exchanged for shares—we discuss which receipts to use for which payments below.

- Bill of Sale for Assets (if incorporating a prior business)
- Receipt of Cash Payment
- Bill of Sale for Transfer of Property
- Receipt for Services Rendered the Corporation
- Receipt for Cancellation of Indebtedness.

Simply make copies of the appropriate forms for your shareholders and prepare them according to the sample forms and instructions below.

✔ The parenthetical blanks, i.e., " _(information)_ ," indicate information that you must complete on the form.

✔ Each circled number (e.g., ❶) refers to a special instruction that provides specific information to help you complete an item. The special instructions immediately follow the sample form.

✔ Fill in the tear-out form using a typewriter or printer with a black-ink ribbon.

a. Prepare a Bill of Sale for Assets If Incorporating a Pre-Existing Business

If you are incorporating a prior business—transferring the assets of an unincorporated business to your corporation in return for the issuance of shares to the prior owners—you may wish to prepare a Bill of Sale to document the transfer of the unincorporated business to the corporation. Complete the Bill of Sale for Assets of a Business as you follow the sample form with instructions below. As indicated in the form, after you fill out the Bill of Sale, attach an inventory of the assets of the prior business that will be transferred to the corporation. If you have any questions, your tax advisor can help you decide on the options offered in this form.

BILL OF SALE FOR ASSETS OF A BUSINESS

This is an agreement between _____ *(names of prior business owner(s))* _____ herein called "transferor(s)," and ____ *(name of corporation)* __ , ❶ a California corporation, herein called "the corporation."

In return for the issuance of ___ *(number of shares)* ___ ❷ shares of stock of the corporation, transferor(s) hereby sell(s), assign(s), and transfer(s) to the corporation all right, title, and interest in the following property:

All the tangible assets listed on the inventory attached to this Bill of Sale and all stock in trade, goodwill, leasehold interests, trade names and other intangible assets [except ___ *(list any nontransferred assets shown here)* ___ ❸] of ___ *(name of prior business)* __ , located at ___ *(address of prior business)* ___ ❹.

In return for the transfer of the above property to it, the corporation hereby agrees to assume, pay, and discharge all debts, duties, and obligations that appear on the books on the date of this agreement and owed on account of said business [except ___ *(any unassumed liabilities shown here)* ___ ❺]. The corporation agrees to indemnify and hold the transferor(s) of said business and their property free from any liability for any such debt, duty, or obligation and from any suits, actions, or legal proceedings brought to enforce or collect any such debt, duty, or obligation.

The transferor(s) hereby appoint(s) the corporation as representative to demand, receive, and collect for itself any and all debts and obligations now owing to said business and hereby assumed by the corporation. The transferor(s) further authorize(s) the corporation to do all things allowed by law to recover and collect any such debts and obligations and to use the transferor's(s') name(s) in such manner as it considers necessary for the collection and recovery of such debts and obligations, provided, however, without cost, expense, or damage to the transferor(s).❻

Dated:_____ ❼   ___ *(signature of prior business owner)* ___ , Transferor
                                                     (typed name)

                                   ___ *(signature of prior business owner)* ___ , Transferor
                                                     (typed name)

Dated:_____ ❼   __ (name of corporation)_____

                          By: ___ (signature of president)___ , President

                                   ___ (signature of treasurer)___ , Treasurer

Special Instructions

❶ Insert the name(s) of the prior business owner(s) in the first blank, followed by the name of your new corporation in the second blank.

❷ Enter the total number of shares to be issued to all prior owners of the business in return for the transfer by them of the prior business to the corporation.

Example: If Patricia and Kathleen will each receive 2,000 shares in return for their respective half-interests in their pre-existing partnership, they would indicate 4,000 shares here.

❸ Use this line to show any assets of the prior business that are not being transferred to the corporation—for example, the owners of the prior business may wish to continue to personally own real estate, and lease it to the new corporation instead of transferring title to the corporation. For most businesses being incorporated, all prior business assets will be transferred to the corporation and you should type "No Exceptions" here. As indicated in this paragraph of the bill of sale, you should attach a current inventory showing the assets of the prior business.

❹ Indicate the name and address of the prior business. For sole proprietorships and partnerships not operating under a fictitious business name, the name(s) of the prior owners may simply be given as the name of the prior business ("Heather Langsley and Chester Langsley"). Otherwise, indicate the trade name, or fictitious business name, of the prior business.

❺ This paragraph indicates that your corporation will assume the liabilities of the prior business. This will be appropriate for the incorporation of most small businesses. In the blank in this paragraph, list any liabilities of the prior business that will *not* be assumed by the corporation. Normally your new corporation will assume *all* liabilities of the prior business and you should indicate "No Exceptions" here. *If your corporation will not assume any of the liabilities of the prior business, make sure to delete this paragraph from your final bill of sale.*

❻ This paragraph allows the corporation to collect for itself any debts and obligations—for example, accounts receivable—owed to the prior business and transferred to the corporation.

❼ Don't date and sign the form yet. You will do this when you distribute the stock certificates to the prior business owners as explained in Section C3 below.

WILL YOU TRANSFER REAL PROPERTY OR LEASES TO YOUR NEW CORPORATION?

If you are transferring real property or a lease to your corporation, you will have to prepare and execute new papers showing corporate ownership, such as deeds, leases, or assignments of leases, prior to issuing shares in exchange for these assets.

When it comes to rental property, you should talk to the landlord about having a new lease prepared showing the corporation as the new tenant. An alternative is to have the prior unincorporated business owners assign the lease to the corporation. However, read your lease carefully before trying to do this—many leases are not assignable without the landlord's permission (although typically, the consent of the landlord cannot be unreasonably withheld).

If the property being transferred is mortgaged, then you will most likely need the permission of the lender to transfer the property. If your real property note agreement contains a "due on sale or transfer" clause, you even may be required to refinance your mortgage if rates have gone up substantially since the existing mortgage was taken out. This, of course, may be so undesirable that you decide not to transfer the real property to the corporation, keeping it instead in the name of the prior business owners, who will lease the property to the new corporation. Also, don't forget that the transfer of real property to your corporation may trigger a Proposition 13 reassessment of the property for tax purposes. For the tax ramifications of transferring real property to your corporation, check with your tax advisor.

An excellent California guide to transferring property interests and preparing new deeds (with tear-out forms) is *The Deeds Book*, by Mary Randolph (Nolo Press).

b. Prepare Cash Receipts

If one or more shareholders will pay cash for shares, you may wish to provide a receipt to the shareholder for the payment as follows:

Special Instructions

❶ Fill in the amount of cash being paid by the shareholder, the name of the shareholder and the number of shares that will be issued to this shareholder.

❷ After you distribute stock certificates as explained in Section C3 below, have the Treasurer date and sign the receipt.

RECEIPT FOR CASH PAYMENT

Receipt of $__(amount of cash payment)__ from __(name of shareholder)__, representing payment in full for __(number of shares)__ shares of the stock of this corporation is hereby acknowledged.❶

Dated:_____❷ _____(name of corporation)_____

By: _____(signature of Treasurer)_____

, Treasurer

---

c. Bill of Sale for Transfer of Property

If specific items of property—other than the assets of an existing business (see subsection a above)—are being transferred to the corporation by a shareholder, prepare a bill of sale for the property as you follow the sample form below. Make sure that the property has first been delivered to the corporation and that any ownership papers (for instance, a "pink slip" for a vehicle) have been signed over to the corporation.

Special Instructions

❶ Show the number of shares being issued to this shareholder and the name of the corporation.

❷ In the empty space below the first paragraph, provide a short description of the property being transferred to the corporation by this shareholder. This description should be brief but specific—for example, vehicle ID and registration number for vehicles, or make, model and serial numbers of other types of property.

❸ After you distribute stock certificates as explained in Section C3 below, have the shareholder date and sign the bill of sale.

BILL OF SALE

In consideration of the issuance of ___(number of shares)___ shares of stock in and by ___(name of corporation)___ ,❶ the undersigned hereby sells, assigns, conveys, transfers and delivers to the corporation all right, title and interest in and to the following property:

(Description of Property)❷

Dated: _____   ❸____(signature of shareholder)____
                                (typed name of shareholder)   ,Transferor

---

d. Receipt for Services Rendered the Corporation

If you will issue shares in return for past services performed by a shareholder for the corporation—remember, in California, you cannot issue shares in return for a promise of the *future* performance of services—prepare the receipt as you follow the sample below.

Special Instructions

❶ Insert the name of the corporation twice and the number of shares the person will receive in return for past performance of services.

❷ In the empty space below the first paragraph, show the date(s), description and value of (amount billed for) the services performed by the shareholder.

❸ After you distribute stock certificates as explained in Section C3 below, have the shareholder date and sign the receipt. In addition, have the shareholder give to the corporation an invoice for these services. After you distribute stock certificates, mark the invoice as "Paid in Full," and have the shareholder date and sign it.

RECEIPT FOR SERVICES RENDERED

In consideration of the performance of the following services actually rendered to, or labor done for, _(name of corporation)_ , the undersigned, who is the provider of such services or labor done, hereby acknowledges the receipt of _(number of shares)_ shares of stock in _(name of corporation)_❶ as payment in full for these services:

(Description of Past Services)❷

Dated:_____❸   _____(signature of shareholder)_____
                                   (typed name of shareholder)

---

e. Receipt for Cancellation of Indebtedness Owed by Corporation to Shareholder

If shares are issued in return for the cancellation of indebtedness owed by the corporation to a shareholder, you may wish prepare a receipt as shown below. Attach a photocopy of the cancelled debt instrument if you have one, such as a promissory note or other written loan agreement, to the receipt.

Special Instructions

❶ Insert the number of shares being issued to the shareholder in return for cancellation of the loan by the shareholder, the name of the corporation, the original date of the loan, and the total of the outstanding principal amount and accrued and unpaid interest (if any) owed by the corporation on the loan on the date the shares will be issued (this is the date the stock certificates will be distributed as explained in Section C3 below).

❷ After you distribute stock certificates as explained in Section C3 below, have the shareholder date and sign the acknowledgment.

ACKNOWLEDGMENT OF CANCELLATION OF INDEBTEDNESS

I acknowledge receipt of ___(number of shares)___ shares of ___(name of corporation)___, for my cancellation of a current loan payable by this corporation to this shareholder, dated ___(date of loan)___, with a remaining unpaid principal amount and unpaid accrued interest, if any, totaling $_(loan balance plus unpaid interest owed on date of stock issuance)_.❶

Dated:_____❷ ____(signature of shareholder)____
                                  (typed name of shareholder)

---

3. Distribute Your Stock Certificates

Now that you've filled in your stock certificates and prepared receipts or bills of sale for your shareholders, the final incorporation step is to issue your shares by distributing your stock certificates to your shareholders. When completing this step, make sure to do the following:

- Wait until you receive payment from each shareholder to distribute that person's shares.
- Date each stock certificate and have your President and Secretary sign each one. (If you have a corporate seal and have not done so yet, impress the corporate seal at the bottom left or right margin of each certificate).
- On your share register, fill in the date in the date of issuance spaces. (If you have are using a corporate records kit from Nolo Press, write the date of issuance in the "Time Became Owner" column.)
- As you receive payment from each shareholder (or, if two persons take title to the shares, the joint shareholders), have that person (or persons) sign

the stock certificate stub. Indicate the date of stock issuance on each stub.
- Complete the date and signature lines on your receipts and/or bills of sale as explained in Section C2 above. Give each shareholder a copy of his or her receipt(s) and/or bill(s) of sale.
- Make sure to place all your completed stock stubs and completed copies of all receipts, bills of sale and any attachments (for instance, an inventory of assets of the prior business, canceled promissory notes and paid-in-full invoices) in your corporate records binder.
- If you have not already done so, make sure to prepare and file your Notice of Stock Transaction with the California Department of Corporations (see Section B above). Remember, you are required to file this Notice form within 15 calendar days of your sale of stock.

CONGRATULATIONS!

You have now completed your last incorporation step!

SIGNING DOCUMENTS FOR THE CORPORATION

There is one last point we wish to make that is central to the operation of your newly formed corporation. One of the reasons you decided to form a corporation was to limit your personal liability in business affairs. So, from now on, whenever you sign a document on behalf of the corporation, be certain to do so in the following manner:

Dated: _____

_____ (name of corporation) _____

By:

_____ (your signature) _____
(type your name), (type your title, such as "President")

   If you fail to sign documents in this manner (on behalf of the corporation in your capacity as a corporate officer or director), you may be leaving yourself open to personal liability for corporate obligations. This is but one example designed to illustrate a basic premise of corporate life: From now on, it is extremely important for you to maintain the distinction between the corporation you've organized and yourself (and the other principals of the corporation). As we've said, your corporation is a separate legal "person" and you want to make sure that other people, businesses, the IRS and the courts respect this distinction.

CHAPTER 7

Finding Helpful Lawyers and Accountants

Even though you can prepare and file standard incorporation forms yourself with little time and trouble, there are times when the expertise of a knowledgeable lawyer and accountant can be invaluable to help you over specific incorporation hurdles. With this in mind, throughout this book we have pointed out various legal and tax questions that can be better resolved with the help of an experienced small business lawyer or tax advisor. In this chapter, we provide common sense guidelines for finding the right lawyer and accountant to help you handle these questions during the course of your incorporation.

A. How to Find the Right Lawyer

Most small businesses can't afford to put a lawyer on retainer (a fee paid in advance to a lawyer to secure routine services for an extended period of time). And even when consulted on an issue-by-issue basis, lawyers' fees mount up fast—way too fast in most instances for legal advice to be affordable for small businesses, except perhaps for the most pressing problems. Just as with individuals, more and more small businesses are trying to at least partially close this legal affordability gap by doing as much of their own legal form preparation as possible. Often a knowledgeable self-help entrepreneur can sensibly accomplish the whole task of incorporation. Other times, it makes sense to briefly consult with a lawyer at an interim stage, or have the paperwork reviewed upon completion.

You obviously don't want a lawyer who is programmed to try and take over all your legal decision-making and form-drafting while running up billable hours as fast as possible. Instead, you need what we call a *legal coach*, someone who is willing to work *with* you—not just *for* you. Under this model, the lawyer helps you take care of many routine incorporation tasks yourself, while being available to consult on more complicated legal issues as the need arises, both during and after your incorporation process.

 YOU DON'T NEED A BIG-TIME CORPORATE LAWYER

There is a lawyer surplus these days, and many newer lawyers especially are open to nontraditional business arrangements. Look for a lawyer with some small business experience, preferably in your field or area of operations. For the most part, you don't want a lawyer who works with big corporations. Not only will this person deal with issues that are far from your concerns, but he or she is almost sure to charge too much.

DON'T ASK A LAWYER FOR TAX ADVICE

When it comes to incorporation decisions that have tax implications, whether deciding if S corporation tax treatment is best for your corporation or choosing the most advantageous employee benefit plan, accountants often have a better grasp of the issues than lawyers. And an added bonus is that, although tax advice doesn't come cheap, accountants often charge less than lawyers.

---

1. Look and Ask Around

When you go looking for a lawyer, don't start with phone books, legal directories or advertisements. Lawyer referral services operated by bar associations are equally unhelpful—they simply supply the names of lawyers who have signed onto the service, often accepting the lawyer's own word for what types of skills he or she has. A better approach is to talk to people in your community who own or operate businesses you respect. Ask them about their lawyer and

what they think of that person's work. If you talk to half a dozen business people, chances are you'll come away with several good leads. Other people, such as your banker, accountant, insurance agent or real estate broker, may be able to provide the names of lawyers they trust to help them with business matters. In addition, friends, relatives, and business associates within your own company may have names of possible lawyers.

 LET YOUR LEGAL COACH REFER YOU TO EXPERTS WHEN NECESSARY

What if you have a very technical legal question? Should you start by seeking out a legal specialist? For starters, the answer is probably no. First, find a good business lawyer to act as your coach. Then rely on this person to suggest specialized materials or experts as the need arises.

2. Talk to the Lawyer Ahead of Time

After you get the names of several good prospects, don't wait until two days before you need to file your Articles or perform another incorporation step before contacting a lawyer. If you do, chances are you'll wind up settling for the first lawyer who can fit you into their schedule—almost a guarantee you'll pay too much for their help.

When you call a lawyer, announce your intentions in advance—that you are looking for a legal coach—someone who is willing to review your papers or answer a specific legal question. Many lawyers will find this request unappealing—for example, they may say they don't feel comfortable reviewing documents you have drafted using self-help materials. If so, thank the person for being frank and call another lawyer. You'll also want to discuss other important issues upfront, such as the lawyer's customary charges for services, as explained further below. No matter what, always trust your instincts and seek a lawyer whose personality and business sense seem compatible with your own.

3. Set the Extent and Cost of Services in Advance

When you hire a lawyer, get a clear understanding of how fees will be computed. Some lawyers bill a flat amount for document review or a specific research problem; others bill to the nearest six- , ten- or twenty-minute interval. Whatever the lawyer's system, you need to understand it. If you feel the quoted fee is too much, don't hesitate to negotiate. When you've found a lawyer whose fees you are comfortable with, it's a good idea to get all fee arrangements—especially those for good-sized jobs—in writing. In California, fee agreements between lawyers and clients must be in writing if the expected fee is $1,000 or more.

USE NON-LAWYER PROFESSIONALS TO CUT DOWN ON LEGAL COSTS

Often non-lawyer professionals perform some tasks better and at less cost than lawyers. For example, look to management consultants for strategic business planning, real estate brokers or appraisers for valuation of properties, brokerage houses for small public or private placements of shares, financial planners for investment advice, accountants for preparation of financial proposals, insurance agents for advice on insurance protection, independent paralegals for routine corporate form-drafting and CPAs for the preparation of tax returns. While each of these matters is likely to have a legal aspect, and you may eventually want to consult your lawyer, normally you won't need to until you've gathered information on your own.

HOW LAWYERS CHARGE FOR LEGAL SERVICES

There are no across-the-board arrangements on how lawyers' fees are to be charged, but you can expect to be charged by one of the following methods:

- **By the hour.** In most parts of the United States, you can get competent services for your small business for $150 to $250 an hour. Newer attorneys still in the process of building a practice may be available for document review, legal research and other types of legal work at lower rates.
- **Flat fee for a specific job.** Under this arrangement, you pay the agreed-upon amount for a given project, regardless of how much or how little time the lawyer spends. Particularly when you first begin working with a lawyer and are worried about hourly costs getting out of control, negotiating a flat fee for a specific job can make sense. For example, the lawyer may review and customize your Bylaws for $300, or review a shareholders' buy-sell agreement (provisions that control how, when and for how much shareholders can sell their shares if they wish to leave the corporation) for $500.
- **Contingent fee based upon settlement amounts or winnings.** This type of fee typically occurs in personal injury, products liability, fraud and discrimination type cases, where a lawsuit will likely be filed. The lawyer gets a percentage of the recovery (often 33%–40%) if you win and nothing if you lose. Since most small business legal needs involve advice and help with drafting paperwork, a contingency fee approach doesn't normally make sense. However, if your business becomes involved in a personal injury claim or lawsuit involving fraud, unfair competition or the infringement of a patent or copyright, you may want to explore the possibility of a contingency fee approach.
- **Retainer.** Some corporations can afford to pay relatively modest amounts, perhaps $1,000 to $2,000 a year, to keep a business lawyer on retainer for ongoing phone or in-person consultations, routine legal form review or preparation, and other business matters during the year. Of course, your retainer won't cover a full-blown legal crisis, but it can help you take care of corporate paperwork (for example, review of initial organizational documents and ongoing contract paperwork) when you need a hand.

4. Confront Any Problems Head-On

If you have any questions about a lawyer's bill or the quality of his or her services, speak up. Buying legal help should be just like purchasing any other consumer service—if you are dissatisfied, seek a reduction in your bill or make it clear that the work needs to be redone properly (for example, better bylaws or a more comprehensive lease). If the lawyer runs a decent business, he or she will promptly and positively deal with your concerns. If you don't get an acceptable response, find another lawyer pronto. If you switch lawyers, you are entitled to get your important documents back from the first lawyer.

Even if you fire your lawyer, you may still feel unjustly wronged. If you can't get satisfaction from the lawyer, write to the client grievance office of the state bar association (with a copy to the lawyer, of course). Often, a phone call from this office to your lawyer will bring the desired results.

FOR MORE INFORMATION

Mad at Your Lawyer, written by Tanya Starnes, a malpractice attorney with over 18 years of experience, and published by Nolo Press, shows how to successfully handle every imaginable problem you could have with a lawyer. It covers:

- what you should reasonably expect from your lawyer
- how lawyers bill for their work and how to handle fee disputes
- how to change lawyers in the middle of a case
- how to file a formal complaint, and if all else fails, how to sue your lawyer.

B. Finding the Right Tax Advisor

Incorporation always involves tax issues, such as whether incorporating will save tax dollars, what corporate tax year is most advantageous to adopt and what the best corporate fringe benefits to provide to the owners-employees of the corporation are. To make good decisions in these and other complicated areas may require the expert advice of a tax advisor. Depending on the issue before you, this advisor may be a certified public accountant, a financial or investment advisor, a corporate loan officer at a bank, a pension plan specialist, or an in-house or outside bookkeeper trained in employment and corporate-tax reporting and return requirements.

Whatever your arrangement, for finding, choosing, using and resolving problems with a tax professional, consider the same issues as those discussed in Section A, above, for legal services. In short, shop around for someone recommended by small business people you respect, or who is otherwise known to you as qualified for the task. Again, you may be able to take advantage of the lower rates offered by newer local practitioners or firms. Your tax person should be available to answer routine questions over the phone, or to handle paperwork and correspondence by mail or fax, with a minimum of formality or ritual. It is likely that you will spend much more time dealing with your tax advisor than your legal advisor, so be particularly attentive to the personal side of this relationship.

Tax issues are often cloudy and subject to a range of interpretations and strategies, so it is absolutely essential that you discuss and agree to the level of tax-aggressiveness you expect from your advisor. Some small business owners want to live on the edge, saving every possible tax dollar, even at the risk that deductions and other tax practices will be challenged by the IRS or state tax agents. Others are willing to pay a bit more in taxes to gain an extra measure of peace of mind. Whatever your tax strategy, make sure you find a tax advisor who feels the same way you do, or is willing to defer to your more liberal or conservative tax tendencies.

As with legal issues that affect your business, it pays to learn as much as you can about corporate and employment taxation. Not only will you have to buy less help from professionals, but you'll be in a good position to make good financial and tax-planning decisions. IRS forms and publications, business and law library books, and trade groups and countless other sources provide accessible information on corporate tax issues. Your accountant or other tax advisor should be able to help you put your hands on good materials. Banks are an excellent source of financial advice, particularly if they will be corporate creditors—after all, they will have a stake in the success of your corporation. Further, the federal Small Business Administration can prove to be an ideal source of financial and tax information and resources (as well as financing in some cases).

RESOURCES FOR TAX AND FINANCIAL INFORMATION

Following are just a few suggestions for finding additional tax and financial information relevant to forming and running your corporation. To get free copies of IRS publications, you can pick them up at your local IRS office or order them by phone (call the toll-free IRS forms and publications request telephone number 1-800-TAX-FORM). Much of this IRS tax material is also available for downloading from the IRS Website at "http://www.irs.gov."

- Start by obtaining *IRS Publication 509, Tax Calendars*, prior to the beginning of each corporate tax year. This pamphlet contains a calendar showing the dates for corporate and employer filings during the year.

- You can find information on withholding, depositing, reporting and paying federal employment taxes in *IRS Publication 15, Circular E, Employer's Tax Guide*, and the Publication 15 Supplement, as well as *IRS Publication 937, Business Reporting*. Also helpful are *IRS Publication 542, Tax Information on Corporations*, and *IRS Publication 334, Tax Guide for Small Business*.

- You'll find helpful information on accounting methods and bookkeeping procedures in *IRS Publication 538, Accounting Periods and Methods*, and *IRS Publication 583, Information for Business Taxpayers*.

- Other helpful sources of tax information include *Small-Time Operator*, by Bernard Kamoroff (Bell Springs Publishing, available through Nolo Press), an excellent primer on business bookkeeping practices that contains ledgers and worksheets, and *Starting Your Business*, by Holmes Crouch (Allyear Tax Guides), an investor and business tax guide.

LEGAL AND TAX RESOURCES FROM NOLO PRESS

Below are a few titles published by Nolo Press that we believe offer valuable legal and tax information to the small business entrepreneur:

- *Legal Guide to Starting and Running a Small Business*, by Fred S. Steingold. This book is an essential resource for every small business owner, whether you are just starting out or are already established. Find out how to form a sole proprietorship, partnership or corporation, negotiate a favorable lease, hire and fire employees, write contracts and resolve business disputes.

- *The Employer's Legal Handbook*, by Fred S. Steingold. Employers need legal advice daily. Here's a comprehensive resource you can refer to over and over again for questions about hiring, firing and everything in between. It covers: safe hiring practices, wage and hour laws, tips and commissions, employee benefits, taxes and liability, insurance, discrimination, sexual harassment and termination.

- *Tax Savvy for Small Business*, by Frederick W. Daily. This book gives business owners information they need about federal taxes and shows them how to make the best tax decisions for their business, maximize their profits and stay out of trouble with the IRS.

- *How to Write a Business Plan*, by Mike McKeever. When you're planning to start a business or raise money to expand an existing one, this book will show you how to write the business plan and loan package necessary to finance your business and make it work. Includes up-to-date sources of financing.

- *How to Create a Buy-Sell Agreement and Control the Destiny of Your Small Business*, by Beth Laurence and Anthony Mancuso. This national title contains step-by-step instructions and forms to prepare a buy-sell agreement for small corporations. The purpose of a buy-sell agreement is to help shareholders keep ownership in the hands of the founders, and to settle the thorny issues of how to buy back shares from departing or deceased owners or their spouses, estates and heirs. The critical issue of how shares of a small, privately held business should be valued when they are bought back by the corporation or the remaining shareholders is also explained in this book. In short, the adoption of a buy-sell agreement is a must for any closely held corporation.

- *Patent It Yourself*, by David Pressman. This state-of-the art guide is a must for any inventor who wants to get a patent—from the patent search to the actual application. Patent attorney and former patent examiner David Pressman covers use and licensing, successful marketing and infringement. This best-selling book is now available in software as well.

- *The Copyright Handbook: How to Protect and Use Written Works*, by Stephen Fishman. Provides forms and step-by-step instructions for protecting all types of written expression under U.S. and international copyright law. It also explains copyright infringement, fair use, works for hire and transfers of copyright ownership.

- *Software Development: A Legal Guide*, by Stephen Fishman. A reference bible for people in the software industry, this book with disk explores the legal ins and outs of copyright, trade secrets and patent protection, employment agreements, working with independent contractors and employees, development and publishing agreements, and multimedia developments.

■

APPENDIX

CALIFORNIA SECRETARY OF STATE INFORMATION

Office hours for all locations are Monday through Friday
8:00 am to 5:00 pm

Corporations Unit

Name Availability Unit   916-654-7960
  (recorded information on how to obtain)
1500 11th Street
Sacramento, CA 95814

Document Filing Support and Legal Review   916-653-2318
1500 11th Street
Sacramento, CA 95814

Information Retrieval and Certification   916-653-2121
1500 11th Street
Sacramento, CA 95814

Status   916-653-7315
  (recorded information on how to obtain)
1500 11th Street
Sacramento, CA 95814

Statement of Officers   916-653-1742
  (filings only)
P.O. Box 944230 (94244-2300)
1500 11th Street
Sacramento, CA 95814

Substituted Service of Process   916-657-5448
  (must be hand delivered)
1500 11th Street
Sacramento, CA 95814

Fresno Branch Office

2497 West Shaw, Suite 101   209-243-2100
Fresno, CA 93711

Los Angeles Branch Office

300 South Spring Street, Room 12513   213-897-3062
Los Angeles, CA 90013-1233

San Diego Branch Office

1350 Front Street, Suite 2060   619-525-4113
San Diego, CA 92101-3690

San Francisco Branch Office

235 Montgomery Street, Suite 725   415-439-6959
San Francisco, CA 94104

BYLAWS

of

_____

ARTICLE I
OFFICES

SECTION 1. PRINCIPAL EXECUTIVE OFFICE

The location of the principal executive office of the corporation shall be fixed by the board of directors. It may be located at any place within or outside the state of California. The secretary of this corporation shall keep the original or a copy of these bylaws, as amended to date, at the principal executive office of the corporation if this office is located in California. If this office is located outside California, the bylaws shall be kept at the principal business office of the corporation within California. The officers of this corporation shall cause the corporation to file an annual statement with the Secretary of State of California as required by Section 1502 of the California Corporations Code specifying the street address of the corporation's principal executive office.

SECTION 2. OTHER OFFICES

The corporation may also have offices at such other places as the board of directors may from time to time designate, or as the business of the corporation may require.

ARTICLE II
SHAREHOLDERS' MEETINGS

SECTION 1. PLACE OF MEETINGS

All meetings of the shareholders shall be held at the principal executive office of the corporation or at such other place as may be determined by the board of directors.

SECTION 2. ANNUAL MEETINGS

The annual meeting of the shareholders shall be held each year on

_____ ,

at which time the shareholders shall elect a board of directors and transact any other proper business. If this date falls on a legal holiday, then the meeting shall be held on the following business day at the same hour.

SECTION 3. SPECIAL MEETINGS

Special meetings of the shareholders may be called by the board of directors, the chairperson of the board of directors, the president, or by one or more shareholders holding at least 10 percent of the voting power of the corporation.

SECTION 4. NOTICES OF MEETINGS

Notices of meetings, annual or special, shall be given in writing to shareholders entitled to vote at the meeting by the secretary or an assistant secretary or, if there be no such officer, or in the case of his or her neglect or refusal, by any director or shareholder.

Such notices shall be given either personally or by first-class mail or other means of written communication, addressed to the shareholder at the address of such shareholder appearing on the stock transfer books of the corporation or given by the shareholder to the corporation for the purpose of notice. Notice shall be given not less than ten (10) nor more than sixty (60) days before the date of the meeting.

Such notice shall state the place, date, and hour of the meeting and (1) in the case of a special meeting, the general nature of the business to be transacted, and that no other business may be transacted, or (2) in the case of an annual meeting, those matters which the board at the time of the mailing of the notice, intends to present for action by the shareholders, but, subject to the provisions of Section 6 of this Article, any proper matter may be presented at the annual meeting for such action. The notice of any meeting at which directors are to be elected shall include the names of the nominees which, at the time of the notice, the board of directors intends to present for election. Notice of any adjourned meeting need not be given unless a meeting is adjourned for forty-five (45) days or more from the date set for the original meeting.

SECTION 5. WAIVER OF NOTICE

The transactions of any meeting of shareholders, however called and noticed, and wherever held, are as valid as though had at a meeting duly held after regular call and notice, if a quorum is present, whether in person or by proxy, and if, either before or after the meeting, each of the persons entitled to vote, not present in person or by proxy, signs a written waiver of notice or a consent to the holding of the meeting or an approval of the minutes thereof. All such waivers or consents shall be filed with the corporate records or made part of the minutes of the meeting. Neither the business to be transacted at the meeting, nor the purpose of any annual or special meeting of shareholders need be specified in any written waiver of notice, except as provided in Section 6 of this Article.

SECTION 6. SPECIAL NOTICE AND WAIVER OF NOTICE REQUIREMENTS

Except as provided below, any shareholder approval at a meeting, with respect to the following proposals, shall be valid only if the general nature of the proposal so approved was stated in the notice of meeting, or in any written waiver of notice:

a. Approval of a contract or other transaction between the corporation and one or more of its directors or between the corporation and any corporation, firm, or association in which one or more of the directors has a material financial interest, pursuant to Section 310 of the California Corporations Code;

b. Amendment of the Articles of Incorporation after any shares have been issued pursuant to Section 902 of the California Corporations Code;

c. Approval of the principal terms of a reorganization pursuant to Section 1201 of the California Corporations Code;

d. Election to voluntarily wind up and dissolve the corporation pursuant to Section 1900 of the California Corporations Code;

e. Approval of a plan of distribution of shares as part of the winding up of the corporation pursuant to Section 2007 of the California Corporations Code.

Approval of the above proposals at a meeting shall be valid with or without such notice, if it is by the unanimous approval of those entitled to vote at the meeting.

SECTION 7. ACTION WITHOUT MEETING

Any action that may be taken at any annual or special meeting of shareholders may be taken without a meeting and without prior notice if a consent, in writing, setting forth the action so taken, shall be signed by the holders of outstanding shares having not less than the minimum number of votes that would be necessary to authorize or take such action at a meeting at which all shares entitled to vote thereon were present and voted.

Unless the consents of all shareholders entitled to vote have been solicited in writing, notice of any shareholders' approval, with respect to any one of the following proposals, without a meeting, by less than unanimous written consent shall be given at least ten (10) days before the consummation of the action authorized by such approval:

a. Approval of a contract or other transaction between the corporation and one or more of its directors or another corporation, firm or association in which one or more of its directors has a material financial interest, pursuant to Section 310 of the California Corporations Code;

b. To indemnify an agent of the corporation pursuant to Section 317 of the California Corporations Code;

c. To approve the principal terms of a reorganization, pursuant to Section 1201 of the California Corporations Code; or

d. Approval of a plan of distribution as part of the winding up of the corporation pursuant to Section 2007 of the California Corporations Code.

Prompt notice shall be given of the taking of any other corporate action approved by shareholders without a meeting by less than a unanimous written consent to those shareholders entitled to vote who have not consented in writing.

Notwithstanding any of the foregoing provisions of this section, and except as provided in Article III, Section 4, of these bylaws, directors may not be elected by written consent except by the unanimous written consent of all shares entitled to vote for the election of directors.

A written consent may be revoked by a writing received by the corporation prior to the time that written consents of the number of shares required to authorize the proposed action have been filed with the secretary of the corporation, but may not be revoked thereafter. Such revocation is effective upon its receipt by the secretary of the corporation.

SECTION 8. QUORUM AND SHAREHOLDER ACTION

A majority of the shares entitled to vote, represented in person or by proxy, shall constitute a quorum at a meeting of shareholders. If a quorum is present, the affirmative vote of the majority of shareholders represented at the meeting and entitled to vote on any matter shall be the act of the shareholders, unless the vote of a greater number is required by law and except as provided in the following paragraphs of this section.

The shareholders present at a duly called or held meeting at which a quorum is present may continue to transact business until adjournment notwithstanding the withdrawal of enough shareholders to leave less than a quorum, if any action is approved by at least a majority of the shares required to constitute a quorum.

In the absence of a quorum, any meeting of shareholders may be adjourned from time to time by the vote of a majority of the shares represented either in person or by proxy, but no other business may be transacted except as provided in the foregoing provisions of this section.

SECTION 9. VOTING

Only shareholders of record on the record date fixed for voting purposes by the board of directors pursuant to Article VIII, Section 3, of these bylaws, or, if there be no such date fixed, on the record dates given below, shall be entitled to vote at a meeting.

If no record date is fixed:

a. The record date for determining shareholders entitled to notice of, or to vote, at a meeting of shareholders, shall be at the close of business on the business day next preceding the day on which notice is given or, if notice is waived, at the close of business on the business day next preceding the day on which the meeting is held.

b. The record date for determining the shareholders entitled to give consent to corporate actions in writing without a meeting, when no prior action by the board is necessary, shall be the day on which the first written consent is given.

c. The record date for determining shareholders for any other purpose shall be at the close of business on the day on which the board adopts the resolution relating thereto, or the 60th day prior to the date of such other action, whichever is later.

Every shareholder entitled to vote shall be entitled to one vote for each share held, except as otherwise provided by law, by the Articles of Incorporation or by other provisions of these bylaws. Except with respect to elections of directors, any shareholder entitled to vote may vote part of his or her shares in favor of a proposal and refrain from voting the remaining shares or vote them against the proposal. If a shareholder fails to specify the number of shares he or she is affirmatively voting, it will be conclusively presumed that the shareholder's approving vote is with respect to all shares the shareholder is entitled to vote.

At each election of directors, shareholders shall not be entitled to cumulate votes unless the candidates' names have been placed in nomination before the commencement of the voting and a shareholder has given notice at the meeting, and before the voting has begun, of his or her intention to cumulate votes. If any shareholder has given such notice, then all shareholders entitled to vote may cumulate their votes by giving one candidate a number of votes equal to the number of directors to be elected multiplied by the number of his or her shares or by distributing such votes on the same principle among any number of candidates as he or she thinks fit. The candidates receiving the highest number of votes, up to the number of directors to be elected, shall be elected. Votes cast against a candidate or which are withheld shall have no effect. Upon the demand of any shareholder made before the voting begins, the election of directors shall be by ballot rather than by voice vote.

SECTION 10. PROXIES

Every person entitled to vote shares may authorize another person or persons to act by proxy with respect to such shares by filing a proxy with the secretary of the corporation. For purposes of these bylaws, a "proxy" means a written authorization signed or an electronic transmission authorized by a shareholder or the shareholder's attorney in fact giving another person or persons power to vote with respect to the shares of the shareholder. "Signed" for the purpose of these bylaws means the placing of the shareholder's name or other authorization on the proxy (whether by manual signature, typewriting, telegraphic, or electronic transmission or otherwise) by the shareholder or the shareholder's attorney in fact. A proxy may be transmitted by an oral telephonic transmission if it is submitted with information from which it may be determined that the proxy was authorized by the shareholder, or his or her attorney in fact.

A proxy shall not be valid after the expiration of eleven (11) months from the date thereof unless otherwise provided in the proxy. Every proxy shall continue in full force and effect until revoked by the person executing it prior to the vote pursuant thereto, except as otherwise provided in Section 705 of the California Corporations Code.

ARTICLE III
DIRECTORS

SECTION 1. POWERS

Subject to any limitations in the Articles of Incorporation and to the provisions of the California Corporations Code, the business and affairs of the corporation shall be managed and all corporate powers shall be exercised by, or under the direction of, the board of directors.

SECTION 2. NUMBER

The authorized number of directors shall be _____ .

After issuance of shares, this bylaw may only be amended by approval of a majority of the outstanding shares entitled to vote; provided, moreover, that a bylaw reducing the fixed number of directors to a number less than five (5) cannot be adopted unless in accordance with the additional requirements of Article IX of these bylaws.

SECTION 3. ELECTION AND TENURE OF OFFICE

The directors shall be elected at the annual meeting of the shareholders and hold office until the next annual meeting and until their successors have been elected and qualified.

SECTION 4. VACANCIES

A vacancy on the board of directors shall exist in the case of death, resignation, or removal of any director or in case the authorized number of directors is increased, or in case the shareholders fail to elect the full authorized number of directors at any annual or special meeting of the shareholders at which any director is elected. The board of directors may declare vacant the office of a director who has been declared of unsound mind by an order of court or who has been convicted of a felony.

Except for a vacancy created by the removal of a director, vacancies on the board of directors may be filled by approval of the board or, if the number of directors then in office is less than a quorum, by (1) the unanimous written consent of the directors then in office, (2) the affirmative vote of a majority of the directors then in office at a meeting held pursuant to notice or waivers of notice complying with this Article of these bylaws, or (3) a sole remaining director. Vacancies occurring on the board by reason of the removal of directors may be filled only by approval of the shareholders. Each director so elected shall hold office until the next annual meeting of the shareholders and until his or her successor has been elected and qualified.

The shareholders may elect a director at any time to fill a vacancy not filled by the directors. Any such election by written consent other than to fill a vacancy created by the removal of a director requires the consent of a majority of the outstanding shares entitled to vote.

Any director may resign effective upon giving written notice to the chairperson of the board of directors, the president, the secretary or to the board of directors unless the notice specifies a later time for the effectiveness of the resignation. If the resignation is effective at a later time, a successor may be elected to take office when the resignation becomes effective. Any reduction of the authorized number of directors does not remove any director prior to the expiration of such director's term in office.

SECTION 5. REMOVAL

Any or all of the directors may be removed without cause if the removal is approved by a majority of the outstanding shares entitled to vote, subject to the provisions of Section 303 of the California Corporations Code. Except as provided in Sections 302, 303 and 304 of the

California Corporations Code, a director may not be removed prior to the expiration of the director's term of office.

The Superior Court of the proper county may, on the suit of shareholders holding at least 10 percent of the number of outstanding shares of any class, remove from office any director in case of fraudulent or dishonest acts or gross abuse of authority or discretion with reference to the corporation and may bar from re-election any director so removed for a period prescribed by the court. The corporation shall be made a party to such action.

SECTION 6. PLACE OF MEETINGS

Meetings of the board of directors shall be held at any place, within or without the State of California, which has been designated in the notice of the meeting or, if not stated in the notice or if there is no notice, at the principal executive office of the corporation or as may be designated from time to time by resolution of the board of directors. Meetings of the board may be held through use of conference telephone, electronic video screen communication or other communications equipment, as long as all of the following apply:

(a) Each member participating in the meeting can communicate with all members concurrently.

(b) Each member is provided the means of participating in all matters before the board, including the capacity to propose, or to interpose, an objection to a specific action to be taken by the corporation.

(c) The corporation adopts and implements some means of verifying both of the following:

(1) A person communicating by telephone, electronic video screen, or other communications equipment is a director entitled to participate in the board meeting.

(2) All statements, questions, actions, or votes were made by that director and not by another person not permitted to participate as a director.

SECTION 7. ANNUAL, REGULAR AND SPECIAL DIRECTORS' MEETINGS

An annual meeting of the board of directors shall be held without notice immediately after and at the same place as the annual meeting of the shareholders.

Other regular meetings of the board of directors shall be held at such times and places as may be fixed from time to time by the board of directors. Call and notice of these regular meetings shall not be required.

Special meetings of the board of directors may be called by the chairperson of the board, the president, vice president, secretary, or any two directors. Special meetings of the board of directors shall be held upon four (4) days' notice by mail, or forty-eight (48) hours' notice delivered personally or by telephone or telegraph or by other electronic means including facsimile or electronic mail message. Mailed notice shall be sent by first-class mail to the director's address that appears on the records of the corporation, or the address given by the director for the purpose of mailing such notice. Notice by voice or facsimile telephone shall be to the telephone number given by a director for such notice. Notice to an electronic mail message system shall be sent to the electronic mail address designated by the director for such mail. A notice or waiver of notice need not specify the purpose of any special meeting of the board of directors.

If any meeting is adjourned for more than 24 hours, notice of the adjournment to another time or place shall be given before the time of the resumed meeting to all directors who were not present at the time of adjournment of the original meeting.

SECTION 8. QUORUM AND BOARD ACTION

A quorum for all meetings of the board of directors shall consist of _____ of the authorized number of directors until changed by amendment to this article of these bylaws.

Every act or decision done or made by a majority of the directors present at a meeting duly held at which a quorum is present is the act of the board, subject to the provisions of Section 310 (relating to the approval of contracts and transactions in which a director has a material financial interest); the provisions of Section 311 (designation of committees); and Section 317(e) (indemnification of directors) of the California Corporations Code. A meeting at which a quorum is initially present may continue to transact business notwithstanding the withdrawal of directors, if any action taken is approved by at least a majority of the required quorum for such meeting.

A majority of the directors present at a meeting may adjourn any meeting to another time and place, whether or not a quorum is present at the meeting.

SECTION 9. WAIVER OF NOTICE

The transactions of any meeting of the board, however called and noticed or wherever held, are as valid as though undertaken at a meeting duly held after regular call and notice if a quorum is present and if, either before or after the meeting, each of the directors not present signs a written waiver of notice, a consent to holding the meeting, or an approval of the minutes thereof. All such waivers, consents, and approvals shall be filed with the corporate records or made a part of the minutes of the meeting. Waivers of notice or consents need not specify the purpose of the meeting.

SECTION 10. ACTION WITHOUT MEETING

Any action required or permitted to be taken by the board may be taken without a meeting, if all members of the board shall individually or collectively consent in writing to such action. Such written consent or consents shall be filed with the minutes of the proceedings of the board. Such action by written consent shall have the same force and effect as a unanimous vote of the directors.

SECTION 11. COMPENSATION

No salary shall be paid directors, as such, for their services but, by resolution, the board of directors may allow a reasonable fixed sum and expenses to be paid for attendance at regular or special meetings. Nothing contained herein shall prevent a director from serving the corporation in any other capacity and receiving compensation therefor. Members of special or standing committees may be allowed like compensation for attendance at meetings.

ARTICLE IV
OFFICERS

SECTION 1. OFFICERS

The officers of the corporation shall be a president, a vice president, a secretary, and a treasurer who shall be the chief financial officer of the corporation. The corporation also may have such other officers with such titles and duties as shall be determined by the board of directors. Any number of offices may be held by the same person.

SECTION 2. ELECTION

All officers of the corporation shall be chosen by, and serve at the pleasure of, the board of directors.

SECTION 3. REMOVAL AND RESIGNATION

An officer may be removed at any time, either with or without cause, by the board. An officer may resign at any time upon written notice to the corporation given to the board, the president, or the secretary of the corporation. Any such resignation shall take effect at the date of receipt of such notice or at any other time specified therein. The removal or resignation of an officer shall be without prejudice to the rights, if any, of the officer or the corporation under any contract of employment to which the officer is a party.

SECTION 4. PRESIDENT

The president shall be the chief executive officer and general manager of the corporation and shall, subject to the direction and control of the board of directors, have general supervision, direction, and control of the business and affairs of the corporation. He or she shall preside at all meetings of the shareholders and directors and be an ex-officio member of all the standing committees, including the executive committee, if any, and shall have the general powers and duties of management usually vested in the office of president of a corporation and shall have such other powers and duties as may from time to time be prescribed by the board of directors or these bylaws.

SECTION 5. VICE PRESIDENT

In the absence or disability of the president, the vice presidents, in order of their rank as fixed by the board of directors (or if not ranked, the vice president designated by the board) shall perform all the duties of the president and, when so acting, shall have all the powers of, and be subject to all the restrictions upon, the president. Each vice president shall have such other powers and perform such other duties as may from time to time be prescribed by the board of directors or these bylaws.

SECTION 6. SECRETARY

The secretary shall keep, or cause to be kept, at the principal executive office of the corporation, a book of minutes of all meetings of directors and shareholders. The minutes shall state the time and place of holding of all meetings; whether regular or special, and if special, how called or authorized; the notice thereof given or the waivers of notice received; the names of those present at directors' meetings; the number of shares present or represented at shareholders' meetings; and an account of the proceedings thereof.

The secretary shall keep, or cause to be kept, at the principal executive office of the corporation, or at the office of the corporation's transfer agent, a share register, showing the names of the shareholders and their addresses, the number and classes of shares held by each, the number and date of certificates issued for shares, and the number and date of cancellation of every certificate surrendered for cancellation.

The secretary shall keep, or cause to be kept, at the principal executive office of the corporation, the original or a copy of the bylaws of the corporation, as amended or otherwise altered to date, certified by him or her.

The secretary shall give, or cause to be given, notice of all meetings of shareholders and directors required to be given by law or by the provisions of these bylaws.

The secretary shall have charge of the seal of the corporation and have such other powers and perform such other duties as may from time to time be prescribed by the board or these bylaws.

In the absence or disability of the secretary, the assistant secretaries if any, in order of their rank as fixed by the board of directors (or if not ranked, the assistant secretary designated by the board of directors), shall have all the powers of, and be subject to all the restrictions upon, the secretary. The assistant secretaries, if any, shall have such other powers and perform such other duties as may from time to time be prescribed by the board of directors or these bylaws.

SECTION 7. TREASURER

The treasurer shall be the chief financial officer of the corporation and shall keep and maintain, or cause to be kept and maintained, adequate and correct books and records of accounts of the properties and business transactions of the corporation.

The treasurer shall deposit monies and other valuables in the name and to the credit of the corporation with such depositories as may be designated by the board of directors. He or she shall disburse the funds of the corporation in payment of the just demands against the corporation as authorized by the board of directors; shall render to the president and directors, whenever they request it, an account of all his or her transactions as treasurer and of the financial condition of the corporation; and shall have such other powers and perform such other duties as may from time to time be prescribed by the board of directors or the bylaws.

In the absence or disability of the treasurer, the assistant treasurers, if any, in order of their rank as fixed by the board of directors (or if not ranked, the assistant treasurer designated by the board of directors), shall perform all the duties of the treasurer and, when so acting, shall have all the powers of and be subject to all the restrictions upon the treasurer. The assistant treasurers, if any, shall have such other powers and perform such other duties as may from time to time be prescribed by the board of directors or these bylaws.

SECTION 8. COMPENSATION

The officers of this corporation shall receive such compensation for their services as may be fixed by resolution of the board of directors.

ARTICLE V
EXECUTIVE COMMITTEES

SECTION 1

The board may, by resolution adopted by a majority of the authorized number of directors, designate one or more committees, each consisting of two or more directors, to serve at the pleasure of the board. Any such committee, to the extent provided in the resolution of the board, shall have all the authority of the board, except with respect to:

a. The approval of any action for which the approval of the shareholders or approval of the outstanding shares is also required.

b. The filling of vacancies on the board or in any committee.

c. The fixing of compensation of the directors for serving on the board or on any committee.

d. The amendment or repeal of bylaws or the adoption of new bylaws.

e. The amendment or repeal of any resolution of the board which by its express terms is not so amendable or repealable.

f. A distribution to the shareholders of the corporation, except at a rate or in a periodic amount or within a price range determined by the board.

g. The appointment of other committees of the board or the members thereof.

ARTICLE VI
CORPORATE RECORDS AND REPORTS

SECTION 1. INSPECTION BY SHAREHOLDERS

The share register shall be open to inspection and copying by any shareholder or holder of a voting trust certificate at any time during usual business hours upon written demand on the corporation, for a purpose reasonably related to such holder's interest as a shareholder or holder of a voting trust certificate. Such inspection and copying under this section may be made in person or by agent or attorney.

The accounting books and records of the corporation and the minutes of proceedings of the shareholders and the board and committees of the board shall be open to inspection upon the written demand of the corporation by any shareholder or holder of a voting trust certificate at any reasonable time during usual business hours, for any proper purpose reasonably related to such holder's interests as a shareholder or as the holder of such voting trust certificate. Such inspection by a shareholder or holder of voting trust certificate may be made in person or by agent or attorney, and the right of inspection includes the right to copy and make extracts.

Shareholders shall also have the right to inspect the original or copy of these bylaws, as amended to date and kept at the corporation's principal executive office, at all reasonable times during business hours.

SECTION 2. INSPECTION BY DIRECTORS

Every director shall have the absolute right at any reasonable time to inspect and copy all books, records, and documents of every kind and to inspect the physical properties of the corporation, domestic or foreign. Such inspection by a director may be made in person or by agent or attorney. The right of inspection includes the right to copy and make extracts.

SECTION 3. RIGHT TO INSPECT WRITTEN RECORDS

If any record subject to inspection pursuant to this chapter is not maintained in written form, a request for inspection is not complied with unless and until the corporation at its expense makes such record available in written form.

SECTION 4. WAIVER OF ANNUAL REPORT

The annual report to shareholders, described in Section 1501 of the California Corporations Code is hereby expressly waived, as long as this corporation has less than 100 holders of record of its shares. This waiver shall be subject to any provision of law, including Section 1501(c) of the California Corporations Code, allowing shareholders to request the corporation to furnish financial statements.

SECTION 5. CONTRACTS, ETC.

The board of directors, except as otherwise provided in the bylaws, may authorize any officer or officers, agent or agents, to enter into any contract or execute any instrument in the name and on behalf of the corporation. Such authority may be general or confined to specific instances. Unless so authorized by the board of directors, no officer, agent, or employee shall have any power or authority to bind the corporation by any contract, or to pledge its credit, or to render it liable for any purpose or to any amount.

ARTICLE VII
INDEMNIFICATION AND INSURANCE OF CORPORATE AGENTS

SECTION 1. INDEMNIFICATION

The directors and officers of the corporation shall be indemnified by the corporation to the fullest extent not prohibited by the California Corporations Code.

SECTION 2. INSURANCE

The corporation shall have the power to purchase and maintain insurance on behalf of any agent (as defined in Section 317 of the California Corporations Code) against any liability asserted against or incurred by the agent in such capacity or arising out of the agent's status as such, whether or not the corporation would have the power to indemnify the agent against such liability under the provisions of Section 317 of the California Corporations Code.

ARTICLE VIII
SHARES

SECTION 1. CERTIFICATES

The corporation shall issue certificates for its shares when fully paid. Certificates of stock shall be issued in numerical order, and shall state the name of the recordholder of the shares represented thereby; the number, designation, if any, and the class or series of shares represented thereby; and contain any statement or summary required by any applicable provision of the California Corporations Code.

Every certificate for shares shall be signed in the name of the corporation by 1) the chairperson or vice chairperson of the board or the president or a vice president and 2) by the treasurer or the secretary or an assistant secretary.

SECTION 2. TRANSFER OF SHARES

Upon surrender to the secretary or transfer agent of the corporation of a certificate for shares duly endorsed or accompanied by proper evidence of succession, assignment, or authority to transfer, it shall be the duty of the secretary of the corporation to issue a new certificate to the person entitled thereto, to cancel the old certificate, and to record the transaction upon the share register of the corporation.

SECTION 3. RECORD DATE

The board of directors may fix a time in the future as a record date for the determination of the shareholders entitled to notice of and to vote at any meeting of shareholders or entitled to receive payment of any dividend or distribution, or any allotment of rights, or to exercise rights in respect to any other lawful action. The record date so fixed shall not be more than sixty (60) days nor less than ten (10) days prior to the date of the meeting nor more than sixty (60) days prior to any other action. When a record date is so fixed, only shareholders of record on that date are entitled to notice of and to vote at the meeting or to receive the dividend, distribution, or allotment of rights, or to exercise the rights as the case may be, notwithstanding any transfer of any shares on the books of the corporation after the record date.

ARTICLE IX
AMENDMENT OF BYLAWS

SECTION 1. BY SHAREHOLDERS

Bylaws may be adopted, amended or repealed by the affirmative vote or by the written consent of holders of a majority of the outstanding shares of the corporation entitled to vote. However, a bylaw amendment which reduces the fixed number of directors to a number less than five (5) shall not be effective if the votes cast against the amendment or the shares not consenting to its adoption are equal to more than 16-2/3 percent of the outstanding shares entitled to vote.

SECTION 2. BY DIRECTORS

Subject to the right of shareholders to adopt, amend or repeal bylaws, the directors may adopt, amend or repeal any bylaw, except that a bylaw amendment changing the authorized number of directors may be adopted by the board of directors only if prior to the issuance of shares.

CERTIFICATE

This is to certify that the foregoing is a true and correct copy of the Bylaws of the corporation named in the title thereto and that such Bylaws were duly adopted by the board of directors of the corporation on the date set forth below.

Dated: _____   _____

                                                      , Secretary

WAIVER OF NOTICE AND CONSENT TO HOLDING OF
FIRST MEETING OF BOARD OF DIRECTORS

of

_____

We, the undersigned, being all the directors of
_____ ,
a California corporation, hereby waive notice of the first meeting of the
board of directors of the corporation and consent to the holding of said
meeting at _____
_____ ,
on _____ , at _____
and consent to the transaction of any and all business by the directors
at the meeting including, without limitation, the adoption of Bylaws, the
election of officers, the selection of the corporation's accounting
period, the designation of the principal executive office of the
corporation, the selection of the place where the corporation's bank
account will be maintained, and the authorization of the sale and
issuance of the initial shares of stock of the corporation.

Dated: _____   _____
                                                          , Director

                             _____
                                                          , Director

                             _____
                                                          , Director

MINUTES OF FIRST MEETING
OF THE BOARD OF DIRECTORS

of

_____

    The board of directors of _____
held its first meeting at _____
on _____ , at _____ .

    The following directors, marked as present next to their names,
were in attendance at the meeting and constituted a quorum of the full
board:

_____	[ ] Present [ ] Absent
_____	[ ] Present [ ] Absent
_____	[ ] Present [ ] Absent

    On motion and by unanimous vote, _____
was elected temporary chairperson and then presided over the meeting.
_____ was elected temporary secretary of the
meeting.

    The chairperson announced that the meeting was held pursuant to
written waiver of notice and consent to holding of the meeting signed by
each of the directors. Upon a motion duly made, seconded, and unanimously
carried, it was resolved that the written waiver of notice and consent to
holding of the meeting be made a part of the minutes of the meeting and
placed in the corporation's minute book.

ARTICLES OF INCORPORATION

    The chairperson announced that the Articles of Incorporation of the
corporation had been filed with the California Secretary of State's
office on _____ .
The chairperson then presented to the meeting a certified copy of the
Articles showing such filing and the secretary was instructed to insert
this copy in the corporation's minute book.

BYLAWS

A proposed set of Bylaws of the corporation was then presented to the meeting for adoption. The Bylaws were considered and discussed and, upon motion duly made and seconded, it was unanimously

RESOLVED, that the Bylaws presented to this meeting be and hereby are adopted as the Bylaws of this corporation;

RESOLVED FURTHER, that the secretary of this corporation be and hereby is directed to execute a Certificate of Adoption of the Bylaws, to insert the Bylaws as so certified in the corporation's minute book and to see that a copy of the Bylaws, similarly certified, is kept at the corporation's principal executive office, as required by law.

ELECTION OF OFFICERS

The chairperson then announced that the next item of business was the election of officers. Upon motion, the following persons were unanimously elected to the following offices, at the annual salaries, if any as determined at the meeting, shown to the right of their names:

President: _____ $ _____

Vice President _____ $ _____

Secretary _____ $ _____

Treasurer _____ $ _____

(Chief Financial Officer)

Each officer who was present accepted his or her office. Thereafter, the President presided at the meeting as chairperson, and the Secretary acted as secretary.

CORPORATE SEAL

The secretary presented to the meeting for adoption a proposed form of seal of the corporation. Upon motion duly made and seconded, it was

RESOLVED, that the form of the corporate seal presented to this meeting be and hereby is adopted as the corporate seal of this corporation, and the secretary of this corporation is directed to place an impression thereof in the space directly next to this resolution.

STOCK CERTIFICATE

The secretary then presented to the meeting for adoption a proposed form of stock certificate for the corporation. Upon motion duly made and seconded, it was

RESOLVED, that the form of stock certificate presented to this meeting be and hereby is adopted for use by this corporation, and the secretary of this corporation is directed to annex a copy thereof to the minutes of this meeting.

SELECTION OF ACCOUNTING PERIOD

The chairperson informed the board that the next order of business was the selection of the accounting period of the corporation. After discussion and upon motion duly made and seconded, it was

RESOLVED, that the accounting period of this corporation shall end on _____ of each year.

LOCATION OF PRINCIPAL EXECUTIVE OFFICE

After discussion as to the exact location of the corporation's principal executive office, upon motion duly made and seconded, it was

RESOLVED, that the principal executive office of this corporation shall be located at _____ .

DESIGNATION OF BANK ACCOUNTS

The chairperson recommended that the corporation open a bank account with _____ .
Upon motion duly made and seconded, it was

RESOLVED, that the funds of this corporation shall be deposited with the bank and branch office indicated just above.

RESOLVED FURTHER, that the Treasurer of this corporation is hereby authorized and directed to establish an account with said bank and to deposit the funds of this corporation therein.

RESOLVED FURTHER, that any officer, employee, or agent of this corporation is hereby authorized to endorse checks, drafts, or other evidences of indebtedness made payable to this corporation, but only for the purpose of deposit.

RESOLVED FURTHER, that all checks, drafts, and other instruments obligating this corporation to pay money shall be signed on behalf of this corporation by any _____ of the following:

_____

_____

_____

_____

_____

RESOLVED FURTHER, that said bank is hereby authorized to honor and pay any and all checks and drafts of this corporation signed as provided herein.

RESOLVED FURTHER, that the authority hereby conferred shall remain in force until revoked by the board of directors of this corporation and until written notice of such revocation shall have been received by said bank.

RESOLVED FURTHER, that the secretary of this corporation be and is hereby authorized to certify as to the continuing authority of these resolutions, the persons authorized to sign on behalf of this corporation, and the adoption of said bank's standard form of resolution, provided that said form does not vary materially from the terms of the foregoing resolutions.

PAYMENT AND DEDUCTION OF ORGANIZATIONAL EXPENSES

The board next considered the question of paying the expenses incurred in the formation of this corporation. A motion was made, seconded and unanimously approved, and it was

RESOLVED, that the President and the Treasurer of this corporation are authorized and empowered to pay all reasonable and proper expenses incurred in connection with the organization of the corporation, including, among others, filing, licensing, and attorney's and accountant's fees, and to reimburse any persons making any such disbursements for the corporation, and it was

FURTHER RESOLVED, that the Treasurer is authorized to elect to deduct on the first federal income tax return of the corporation the foregoing expenditures ratably over a sixty-month period starting in the month the corporation begins its business, pursuant to, and to the extent permitted by, Section 248 of the Internal Revenue Code of 1986, as amended.

ELECTION OF FEDERAL S CORPORATION TAX TREATMENT

The board of directors next considered the advantages of electing to be taxed under the provisions of Subchapter S of the Internal Revenue Code of 1986, as amended. After discussion, upon motion duly made and seconded, it was unanimously

RESOLVED, that this corporation hereby elects to be treated as a Small Business Corporation for federal income tax purposes under Subchapter S of the Internal Revenue Code of 1986, as amended.

RESOLVED FURTHER, that the officers of this corporation take all actions necessary and proper to effectuate the foregoing resolution, including, among other things, obtaining the requisite consents from the shareholders of this corporation and executing and filing the appropriate forms with the Internal Revenue Service within the time limits specified by law.

QUALIFICATION OF STOCK AS SECTION 1244 STOCK

The board next considered the advisability of qualifying the stock of this corporation as Section 1244 Stock as defined in Section 1244 of the Internal Revenue Code of 1986, as amended, and of organizing and managing the corporation so that it is a Small Business Corporation as defined in that section. Upon motion duly made and seconded, it was unanimously

RESOLVED, that the proper officers of the corporation are, subject to the requirements and restrictions of federal, California and any other applicable securities laws, authorized to sell and issue shares of stock in return for the receipt of an aggregate amount of money and other property, as a contribution to capital and as paid-in surplus, which does not exceed $1,000,000.

RESOLVED FURTHER, that the sale and issuance of shares shall be conducted in compliance with Section 1244 so that the corporation and its shareholders may obtain the benefits of that section.

RESOLVED FURTHER, that the proper officers of the corporation are directed to maintain such records as are necessary pursuant to Section 1244 so that any shareholder who experiences a loss on the transfer of shares of stock of the corporation may determine whether he or she qualifies for ordinary loss deduction treatment on his or her individual income-tax return.

AUTHORIZATION OF ISSUANCE OF SHARES

The board of directors next took up the matter of the sale and issuance of stock to provide capital for the corporation. Upon motion duly made and seconded, it was unanimously

RESOLVED, that the corporation sell and issue the following number of its authorized common shares to the following persons, in the amounts and for the consideration set forth under their names below. The board also hereby determines that the fair value to the corporation of any consideration for such shares issued other than for money is as set forth below:

Name	Number of Shares	Consideration	Fair Value
_____	_____	_____	$_____
_____	_____	_____	$_____
_____	_____	_____	$_____
_____	_____	_____	$_____
_____	_____	_____	$_____
_____	_____	_____	$_____
_____	_____	_____	$_____
_____	_____	_____	$_____
_____	_____	_____	$_____
_____	_____	_____	$_____

RESOLVED FURTHER, that these shares shall be sold and issued by this corporation strictly in accordance with the terms of the exemption from qualification of these shares as provided for in Section 25102(f) of the California Corporations Code.

RESOLVED FURTHER, that the appropriate officers of this corporation are hereby authorized and directed to take such actions and execute such documents as they may deem necessary or appropriate to effectuate the sale and issuance of such shares for such consideration.

Since there was no further business to come before the meeting, upon motion duly made and seconded, the meeting was adjourned.

_____

, Secretary

SHAREHOLDER REPRESENTATION LETTER

To: _____

_____

_____

I, _____ , in connection with my purchase of _____ common shares of the corporation named above, hereby make the following representations:

A. I am a suitable purchaser of these shares under the California limited offering exemption because:

1. [ ] I am a director, officer or promoter of the corporation, or because I occupy a position with the corporation with duties and authority substantially similar to those of an executive officer of the corporation.

2. [ ] I have a pre-existing personal and/or business relationship with the corporation, or one or more of its directors, officers or controlling persons, consisting of personal or business contacts of a nature and duration which enables me to be aware of the character, business acumen and general business and financial circumstances of the person (including the corporation) with whom such relationship exists.

3. [ ] I have the capacity to protect my own interests in connection with my purchase of the above shares by reason of my own business and/or financial experience.

4(a). [ ] Pursuant to Section 260.102.13(e) of Title 10 of the California Code of Regulations, I am purchasing $150,000 or more of the corporation's shares, and either 1) my investment (including mandatory assessments) does not exceed 10% of my net worth or joint net worth with my spouse, or 2) by reason of my own business and/or financial experience, or the business and/or financial experience of my professional advisor (who is unaffiliated with and not compensated by the corporation or any of its affiliates or selling agents), I have, or my professional advisor has, the capacity to protect my own interests in connection with the purchase of these shares.

4(b). [ ] Pursuant to Section 260.102.13(g) of Title 10 of the California Code of Regulations, I am an "accredited investor" under Rule 501(a) of Regulation D adopted by the Securities and Exchange Commission under the Securities Act of 1933. This means either 1) my individual net worth, or joint net worth with my spouse, at the time of the purchase of these shares, exceeds $ 1,000,000; 2) my individual income is in excess of $200,000 in each of the two most recent years or my joint income with my spouse is in excess of $300,000 in each of those years, and I have a reasonable expectation of reaching the same income level in the current year; or 3) I qualify under one of the other accredited investor categories of Rule 501(a) of SEC Regulation D.

5(a). [ ]   I have the capacity to protect my own interests in connection with my purchase of the above shares by reason of the business and/or financial experience of _____ , whom I have engaged and hereby designate as my professional advisor in connection with my purchase of the above shares.

5(b).   REPRESENTATION OF PROFESSIONAL ADVISOR

_____ hereby represents:

(1) I have been engaged as the professional advisor of _____ and have provided him or her with investment advice in connection with the purchase of _____ common shares in _____ .

(2) As a regular part of my business as a/an _____ _____ I am customarily relied upon by others for investment recommendations or decisions and I am customarily compensated for such services, either specifically or by way of compensation for related professional services.

(3) I am unaffiliated with and am not compensated by the corporation or any affiliate or selling agent of the corporation, directly or indirectly. I do not have, nor will I have (a) a relationship of employment with the corporation, either as an employee, employer, independent contractor or principal; (b) the beneficial ownership of securities of the corporation, its affiliates or selling agents, in excess of 1% of its securities; or (c) a relationship with the corporation such that I control, am controlled by, or am under common control with the corporation, and, more specifically, a relationship by which I possess, directly or indirectly, the power to direct, or cause the direction, of the management, policies or actions of the corporation.

Dated: _____   _____
                                     , Professional Advisor

6. [ ] I am the spouse, relative, or relative of the spouse of another purchaser of shares and I have the same principal residence as this purchaser.

B. I represent that I am purchasing these shares for investment for my own account and not with a view to, or for, sale in connection with any distribution of the shares. I understand that these shares have not been qualified or registered under any state or federal securities law and that they may not be transferred or otherwise disposed of without such qualification or registration pursuant to such laws or an opinion of legal counsel satisfactory to the corporation that such qualification or registration is not required.

C. I have not received any advertisement or general solicitation with respect to the sale of the shares of the above named corporation.

D. I represent that, before signing this document, I have been provided access to, or been given, all material facts relevant to the purchase of my shares, including all financial and written information about the corporation and the terms and conditions of the stock offering and that I have been given the opportunity to ask questions and receive answers concerning any additional terms and conditions of the stock offering or other information which I, or my professional advisor if I have designated one, felt necessary to protect my interests in connection with the stock purchase transaction.

Dated: _____   _____

Department of Corporations File No., if any
_____
(Insert File Number(s) of Previous Filings
Before the Department, if any)

FEE: $25.00 $35.00 $50.00 $150.00 $300.00
(Circle the appropriate amount of fee.
See Corp. Code Section 25608(c))

COMMISSIONER OF CORPORATIONS
STATE OF CALIFORNIA

NOTICE OF TRANSACTION PURSUANT TO CORPORATIONS CODE SECTION 25102(f)

A. Check one: Transaction under [ ] Section 25102(f)   [ ] Rule 260.103.

1. Name of Issuer: _____

2. Address of Issuer: _____
                          Street   City   State   ZIP

    Mailing Address: _____
                          Street   City   State   ZIP

3. Area Code and Telephone Number: _____

4. Issuer's state (or other jurisdiction) of incorporation or organization: _____
_____

5. Title of class or classes of securities sold in transaction: _____
_____

6. The value of the securities sold or proposed to be sold in the transaction,
determined in accordance with Corp. Code Sec. 25608(g) in connection with the fee
required upon filing this notice, is (fee based on amount shown in line (iii) under
"Total Offering"):

	California	Total Offering
(a) (i) in money	$_____	$_____
(ii) in consideration other than money	$_____	$_____
(iii) total of (i) and (ii)	$_____	$_____

    (b)   ( ) Change in rights, preferences, privileges or restrictions of or
                 on outstanding securities. ($25.00 fee)   (See Rule 260.103)

7. Type of filing under Securities Act of 1933, if applicable: _____
_____

8. Date of Notice: _____   _____

                                                          Issuer

( ) Check if issuer already has a   _____
     consent to service of process   Authorized Signature on behalf of issuer
     on file with the Commissioner.

                                            _____
                                            Print name and title of signatory

Name, Address and Phone number of contact person:

_____

_____

_____

Instruction: Each issuer (other than a California corporation) filing a notice under
Section 25102(f) must file a consent to service of process (Form 260.165), unless it
already has a consent to service on file with the Commissioner.

260.102.14(c)   (10/84)

BILL OF SALE FOR ASSETS OF A BUSINESS

This is an agreement between:

_____

_____

_____ ,

herein called "transferor(s)," and _____

_____ ,

a California corporation, herein called "the corporation."

In return for the issuance of _____
shares of stock of the corporation, transferor(s) hereby sell(s),
assign(s), and transfer(s) to the corporation all right, title, and
interest in the following property:

All the tangible assets listed on the inventory attached to this
Bill of Sale and all stock in trade, goodwill, leasehold interests, trade
names, and other intangible assets except _____

_____

_____

_____

_____

of _____ , located at

_____ .

In return for the transfer of the above property to it, the
corporation hereby agrees to assume, pay, and discharge all debts,
duties, and obligations that appear on the date of this agreement on
the books and owed on account of said business except _____

_____

_____

_____

_____ .

The corporation agrees to indemnify and hold the transferor(s) of said
business and their property free from any liability for any such debt,
duty, or obligation and from any suits, actions, or legal proceedings
brought to enforce or collect any such debt, duty, or obligation.

The transferor(s) hereby appoint(s) the corporation as
representative to demand, receive, and collect for itself any and all
debts and obligations now owing to said business and hereby assumed by
the corporation. The transferor(s) further authorize(s) the corporation

to do all things allowed by law to recover and collect any such debts and obligations and to use the transferor's(s') name(s) in such manner as it considers necessary for the collection and recovery of such debts and obligations, provided, however, without cost, expense, or damage to the transferor(s).

Dated: _____   _____

                                                            , Transferor

                            _____

                                                            , Transferor

                            _____

                                                            , Transferor

Dated: _____   _____

                      By: _____

                                                            , President

                            _____

                                                            , Treasurer

RECEIPT FOR CASH PAYMENT

Receipt of $ _____ from

_____ ,

representing payment in full for _____ shares of the stock of this

corporation is hereby acknowledged.

Dated: _____   _____

                                Name of Corporation

                    By: _____

                                     , Treasurer

ACKNOWLEDGEMENT FOR CANCELLATION OF INDEBTEDNESS

I acknowledge receipt of _____ shares of _____

_____

for my cancellation of a current outstanding loan payable by this

corporation to this shareholder, dated _____,with a remaining unpaid

principal amount and unpaid accrued interest, if any, totaling

$_____.

Dated: _____   _____

BILL OF SALE FOR ITEMS OF PROPERTY

In consideration of the issuance of _____

shares of stock in and by _____ ,

the undersigned hereby sells, assigns, conveys, transfers, and delivers

to the corporation all right, title and interest in and to the following

property:

Dated: _____   _____

                                              , Transferor

RECEIPT FOR SERVICES RENDERED

In consideration of the performance of the following services actually rendered to, or labor done for _____ , the undersigned, the provider of such services or labor done, hereby acknowledges the receipt of _____ shares of stock in _____ as payment in full for these services:

Dated: _____   _____

Share Register

Certificate Number	Number	Date of Issuance			Shareholder's Name and Address	Amount Paid
		Month	Day	Year		

Share Register

Certificate Number	Number	Date of Issuance			Shareholder's Name and Address	Amount Paid
		Month	Day	Year		

Transfer Ledger

Transfer Date			Transferee's Name and Address	Certificate Reissued		Certificate Surrendered	
Month	Day	Year		No.	Number of Shares	No.	Number of Shares

Transfer Ledger

Transfer Date			Transferee's Name and Address	Certificate Reissued		Certificate Surrendered	
Month	Day	Year		No.	Number of Shares	No.	Number of Shares

NUMBER _____   SHARES _____

INCORPORATED UNDER THE LAWS OF CALIFORNIA
Common Shares

THE SHARES REPRESENTED BY THIS CERTIFICATE HAVE NOT BEEN REGISTERED OR QUALIFIED UNDER ANY FEDERAL OR STATE SECURITIES LAW. THEY HAVE BEEN ACQUIRED FOR INVESTMENT PURPOSES AND NOT WITH A VIEW TOWARD RESALE AND MAY NOT BE OFFERED FOR SALE, SOLD, TRANSFERRED, OR PLEDGED WITHOUT REGISTRATION AND QUALIFICATION PURSUANT TO SUCH LAWS OR AN OPINION OF LEGAL COUNSEL SATISFACTORY TO THE CORPORATION THAT SUCH REGISTRATION AND QUALIFICATION IS NOT REQUIRED.

This Certifies that _____ *is the owner of* _____ *fully paid and non-assessable Shares of the above Corporation transferable only on the books of the Corporation by the holder hereof in person or by duly authorized Attorney upon surrender of this Certificate properly endorsed.*

In Witness Whereof, the Corporation has caused this Certificate to be signed by its duly authorized officers and to be sealed with the Seal of the Corporation.

Dated _____

_____, *President*   _____, *Secretary*

For value received, the undersigned hereby sells, assigns and

transfers to _____

_____

_____ *Shares*

represented by the within Certificate, and does hereby irrevocably

constitute and appoint _____

Attorney to transfer the said shares on the books of the within-

named Corporation with full power of substitution in the premises.

Dated: _____

    In presence of _____

_____

NOTICE: The signature to this assignment must correspond with the name as written upon the face of this certificate in every particular without alteration or enlargement, or any change whatever.

For value received, the undersigned hereby sells, assigns and transfers to _____

PRINT OR TYPE NAME AND ADDRESS OF ASSIGNEE

_____

_____ *Shares*

represented by the within Certificate, and does hereby irrevocably constitute and appoint _____

Attorney to transfer the said shares on the books of the within-named Corporation with full power of substitution in the premises.

Dated: _____

In presence of _____

_____

NOTICE: The signature to this assignment must correspond with the name as written upon the face of this certificate in every particular without alteration or enlargement, or any change whatever.

NUMBER _____

SHARES _____

INCORPORATED UNDER THE LAWS OF CALIFORNIA

Common Shares

THE SHARES REPRESENTED BY THIS CERTIFICATE HAVE NOT BEEN REGISTERED OR QUALIFIED UNDER ANY FEDERAL OR STATE SECURITIES LAW. THEY HAVE BEEN ACQUIRED FOR INVESTMENT PURPOSES AND NOT WITH A VIEW TOWARD RESALE AND MAY NOT BE OFFERED FOR SALE, SOLD, TRANSFERRED, OR PLEDGED WITHOUT REGISTRATION AND QUALIFICATION PURSUANT TO SUCH LAWS OR AN OPINION OF LEGAL COUNSEL SATISFACTORY TO THE CORPORATION THAT SUCH REGISTRATION AND QUALIFICATION IS NOT REQUIRED.

This Certifies that _____ *is the owner of* _____ *fully paid and non-assessable Shares of the above Corporation transferable only on the books of the Corporation by the holder hereof in person or by duly authorized Attorney upon surrender of this Certificate properly endorsed.*

In Witness Whereof, the Corporation has caused this Certificate to be signed by its duly authorized officers and to be sealed with the Seal of the Corporation.

Dated _____

_____, *President*

_____, *Secretary*

For value received, the undersigned hereby sells, assigns and transfers to _____

PRINT OR TYPE NAME AND ADDRESS OF ASSIGNEE

_____

_____ *Shares*

represented by the within Certificate, and does hereby irrevocably constitute and appoint _____

Attorney to transfer the said shares on the books of the within-named Corporation with full power of substitution in the premises.

Dated: _____

In presence of _____

_____

NOTICE: The signature to this assignment must correspond with the name as written upon the face of this certificate in every particular without alteration or enlargement, or any change whatever.

NUMBER ___

SHARES ___

INCORPORATED UNDER THE LAWS OF CALIFORNIA

Common Shares

THE SHARES REPRESENTED BY THIS CERTIFICATE HAVE NOT BEEN REGISTERED OR QUALIFIED UNDER ANY FEDERAL OR STATE SECURITIES LAW. THEY HAVE BEEN ACQUIRED FOR INVESTMENT PURPOSES AND NOT WITH A VIEW TOWARD RESALE AND MAY NOT BE OFFERED FOR SALE, SOLD, TRANSFERRED, OR PLEDGED WITHOUT REGISTRATION AND QUALIFICATION PURSUANT TO SUCH LAWS OR AN OPINION OF LEGAL COUNSEL SATISFACTORY TO THE CORPORATION THAT SUCH REGISTRATION AND QUALIFICATION IS NOT REQUIRED.

This Certifies that ___ *is the owner of* ___ *fully paid and non-assessable Shares of the above Corporation transferable only on the books of the Corporation by the holder hereof in person or by duly authorized Attorney upon surrender of this Certificate properly endorsed.*

In Witness Whereof, the Corporation has caused this Certificate to be signed by its duly authorized officers and to be sealed with the Seal of the Corporation.

Dated ___

___, *President*

___, *Secretary*

For value received, the undersigned hereby sells, assigns and transfers to _____

PRINT OR TYPE NAME AND ADDRESS OF ASSIGNEE

_____

_____ *Shares*

represented by the within Certificate, and does hereby irrevocably constitute and appoint _____

Attorney to transfer the said shares on the books of the within-named Corporation with full power of substitution in the premises.

Dated: _____

In presence of _____

_____

NOTICE: The signature to this assignment must correspond with the name as written upon the face of this certificate in every particular without alteration or enlargement, or any change whatever.

For value received, the undersigned hereby sells, assigns and transfers to _____

PRINT OR TYPE NAME AND ADDRESS OF ASSIGNEE

_____

_____ *Shares*

represented by the within Certificate, and does hereby irrevocably constitute and appoint _____

Attorney to transfer the said shares on the books of the within-named Corporation with full power of substitution in the premises.

Dated: _____

        In presence of _____

_____

NOTICE: The signature to this assignment must correspond with the name as written upon the face of this certificate in every particular without alteration or enlargement, or any change whatever.

NUMBER _____

SHARES _____

INCORPORATED UNDER THE LAWS OF CALIFORNIA

Common Shares

THE SHARES REPRESENTED BY THIS CERTIFICATE HAVE NOT BEEN REGISTERED OR QUALIFIED UNDER ANY FEDERAL OR STATE SECURITIES LAW. THEY HAVE BEEN ACQUIRED FOR INVESTMENT PURPOSES AND NOT WITH A VIEW TOWARD RESALE AND MAY NOT BE OFFERED FOR SALE, SOLD, TRANSFERRED, OR PLEDGED WITHOUT REGISTRATION AND QUALIFICATION PURSUANT TO SUCH LAWS OR AN OPINION OF LEGAL COUNSEL SATISFACTORY TO THE CORPORATION THAT SUCH REGISTRATION AND QUALIFICATION IS NOT REQUIRED.

This Certifies that _____ *is the owner of* _____ *fully paid and non-assessable Shares of the above Corporation transferable only on the books of the Corporation by the holder hereof in person or by duly authorized Attorney upon surrender of this Certificate properly endorsed.*

In Witness Whereof, the Corporation has caused this Certificate to be signed by its duly authorized officers and to be sealed with the Seal of the Corporation.

Dated _____

_____ , *President*

_____ , *Secretary*

For value received, the undersigned hereby sells, assigns and transfers to _____

PRINT OR TYPE NAME AND ADDRESS OF ASSIGNEE

_____

_____ *Shares*

represented by the within Certificate, and does hereby irrevocably constitute and appoint _____

Attorney to transfer the said shares on the books of the within-named Corporation with full power of substitution in the premises.

Dated: _____

In presence of _____

_____

NOTICE: The signature to this assignment must correspond with the name as written upon the face of this certificate in every particular without alteration or enlargement, or any change whatever.

Left stub (transfer record):

Certificate Number _____

For _____ Shares

Issued To:

Dated _____, _____

From Whom Transferred

Dated _____, _____

No. Original Shares	No. Original Certificate	No. of Shares Transferred

Received Certificate Number _____

For _____ Shares

This _____ day of _____, _____

_____
SIGNATURE

Certificate:

NUMBER _____

SHARES _____

INCORPORATED UNDER THE LAWS OF CALIFORNIA

Common Shares

THE SHARES REPRESENTED BY THIS CERTIFICATE HAVE NOT BEEN REGISTERED OR QUALIFIED UNDER ANY FEDERAL OR STATE SECURITIES LAW. THEY HAVE BEEN ACQUIRED FOR INVESTMENT PURPOSES AND NOT WITH A VIEW TOWARD RESALE AND MAY NOT BE OFFERED FOR SALE, SOLD, TRANSFERRED, OR PLEDGED WITHOUT REGISTRATION AND QUALIFICATION PURSUANT TO SUCH LAWS OR AN OPINION OF LEGAL COUNSEL SATISFACTORY TO THE CORPORATION THAT SUCH REGISTRATION AND QUALIFICATION IS NOT REQUIRED.

This Certifies that _____ is the owner of _____ fully paid and non-assessable Shares of the above Corporation transferable only on the books of the Corporation by the holder hereof in person or by duly authorized Attorney upon surrender of this Certificate properly endorsed.

In Witness Whereof, the Corporation has caused this Certificate to be signed by its duly authorized officers and to be sealed with the Seal of the Corporation.

Dated _____

_____, President

_____, Secretary

For value received, the undersigned hereby sells, assigns and transfers to _____

PRINT OR TYPE NAME AND ADDRESS OF ASSIGNEE

_____

_____ *Shares*

represented by the within Certificate, and does hereby irrevocably constitute and appoint _____

Attorney to transfer the said shares on the books of the within-named Corporation with full power of substitution in the premises.

Dated: _____

In presence of _____

_____

NOTICE: The signature to this assignment must correspond with the name as written upon the face of this certificate in every particular without alteration or enlargement, or any change whatever.

Certificate Number _____

For _____ Shares

Issued To:

_____ , _____

Dated _____

From Whom Transferred

Dated _____ , _____

No. Original Shares	No. Original Certificate	No. of Shares Transferred

---

Received Certificate Number _____

For _____

This _____ day of _____ , _____

SIGNATURE

NUMBER _____

SHARES _____

INCORPORATED UNDER THE LAWS OF CALIFORNIA

Common Shares

THE SHARES REPRESENTED BY THIS CERTIFICATE HAVE NOT BEEN REGISTERED OR QUALIFIED UNDER ANY FEDERAL OR STATE SECURITIES LAW. THEY HAVE BEEN ACQUIRED FOR INVESTMENT PURPOSES AND NOT WITH A VIEW TOWARD RESALE AND MAY NOT BE OFFERED FOR SALE, SOLD, TRANSFERRED, OR PLEDGED WITHOUT REGISTRATION AND QUALIFICATION PURSUANT TO SUCH LAWS OR AN OPINION OF LEGAL COUNSEL SATISFACTORY TO THE CORPORATION THAT SUCH REGISTRATION AND QUALIFICATION IS NOT REQUIRED.

This Certifies that _____ *is the owner of* _____ *fully paid and non-assessable Shares of the above Corporation transferable only on the books of the Corporation by the holder hereof in person or by duly authorized Attorney upon surrender of this Certificate properly endorsed.*

In Witness Whereof, the Corporation has caused this Certificate to be signed by its duly authorized officers and to be sealed with the Seal of the Corporation.

Dated _____

_____ , *President*

_____ , *Secretary*

For value received, the undersigned hereby sells, assigns and transfers to _____

PRINT OR TYPE NAME AND ADDRESS OF ASSIGNEE

_____

_____ *Shares represented by the within Certificate, and does hereby irrevocably constitute and appoint* _____
Attorney to transfer the said shares on the books of the within-named Corporation with full power of substitution in the premises.
Dated: _____

In presence of _____

_____

NOTICE: The signature to this assignment must correspond with the name as written upon the face of this certificate in every particular without alteration or enlargement, or any change whatever.

Certificate Number _____

For _____ Shares

Issued To:

_____

Dated _____, _____,

From Whom Transferred

Dated _____, _____,

No. Original Shares	No. Original Certificate	No. of Shares Transferred

---

Received Certificate Number _____

For _____

This _____ day of _____, _____

SIGNATURE _____

NUMBER _____   SHARES _____

INCORPORATED UNDER THE LAWS OF CALIFORNIA
Common Shares

THE SHARES REPRESENTED BY THIS CERTIFICATE HAVE NOT BEEN REGISTERED OR QUALIFIED UNDER ANY FEDERAL OR STATE SECURITIES LAW. THEY HAVE BEEN ACQUIRED FOR INVESTMENT PURPOSES AND NOT WITH A VIEW TOWARD RESALE AND MAY NOT BE OFFERED FOR SALE, SOLD, TRANSFERRED, OR PLEDGED WITHOUT REGISTRATION AND QUALIFICATION PURSUANT TO SUCH LAWS OR AN OPINION OF LEGAL COUNSEL SATISFACTORY TO THE CORPORATION THAT SUCH REGISTRATION AND QUALIFICATION IS NOT REQUIRED.

This Certifies that _____ *is the owner of* _____ *fully paid and non-assessable Shares of the above Corporation transferable only on the books of the Corporation by the holder hereof in person or by duly authorized Attorney upon surrender of this Certificate properly endorsed.*

In Witness Whereof, the Corporation has caused this Certificate to be signed by its duly authorized officers and to be sealed with the Seal of the Corporation.

Dated _____

_____, *President*

_____, *Secretary*

For value received, the undersigned hereby sells, assigns and transfers to _____

PRINT OR TYPE NAME AND ADDRESS OF ASSIGNEE

_____

_____ *Shares*

represented by the within Certificate, and does hereby irrevocably constitute and appoint _____

Attorney to transfer the said shares on the books of the within-named Corporation with full power of substitution in the premises.

Dated: _____

In presence of _____

_____

NOTICE: The signature to this assignment must correspond with the name as written upon the face of this certificate in every particular without alteration or enlargement, or any change whatever.

NUMBER _____   SHARES _____

INCORPORATED UNDER THE LAWS OF CALIFORNIA

Common Shares

THE SHARES REPRESENTED BY THIS CERTIFICATE HAVE NOT BEEN REGISTERED OR QUALIFIED UNDER ANY FEDERAL OR STATE SECURITIES LAW. THEY HAVE BEEN ACQUIRED FOR INVESTMENT PURPOSES AND NOT WITH A VIEW TOWARD RESALE AND MAY NOT BE OFFERED FOR SALE, SOLD, TRANSFERRED, OR PLEDGED WITHOUT REGISTRATION AND QUALIFICATION PURSUANT TO SUCH LAWS OR AN OPINION OF LEGAL COUNSEL SATISFACTORY TO THE CORPORATION THAT SUCH REGISTRATION AND QUALIFICATION IS NOT REQUIRED.

This Certifies that _____ *is the owner of* _____ *fully paid and non-assessable Shares of the above Corporation transferable only on the books of the Corporation by the holder hereof in person or by duly authorized Attorney upon surrender of this Certificate properly endorsed.*

In Witness Whereof, the Corporation has caused this Certificate to be signed by its duly authorized officers and to be sealed with the Seal of the Corporation.

Dated _____, *President*

_____, *Secretary*

For value received, the undersigned hereby sells, assigns and transfers to _____

PRINT OR TYPE NAME AND ADDRESS OF ASSIGNEE

_____

_____ *Shares*

represented by the within Certificate, and does hereby irrevocably constitute and appoint _____

Attorney to transfer the said shares on the books of the within-named Corporation with full power of substitution in the premises.

Dated: _____

In presence of _____

_____

NOTICE: The signature to this assignment must correspond with the name as written upon the face of this certificate in every particular without alteration or enlargement, or any change whatever.

Index

THE NOLO ADVANTAGE™ RECORDS KIT

It's easy to keep your corporate records well-organized with the Nolo Advantage™ Corporate Records Kit.

Each kit contains: (see * below)

- **Corporate Records Binder** • A handsome padded vinyl three-ring binder.

- **20 Stock Certificates** • These stock certificates are customized are customized with your corporation's name and state of formation.

- **Index Dividers** for your Articles, Bylaws, Minutes and Stock Certificates

- **Share Register,** and **Stock Transfer Ledger**

- **Special Instructions** prepared by Attorney Anthony Mancuso on how to use each section of your corporate records book.

* *Optional Metal Corporate Seal* • Shows the name of your corporation and date of formation. The corporate seal is a solid metal embossing tool, and, although not legally required, many corporations use it to indicate that a document is the duly authorized act of the corporation.

ORDER COUPON

Nolo Advantage™ Corporate Records Kit

Name of Corporation - Please print the corporate name exactly as it appears on your Articles making sure Capital and lower case letters are clear and the spelling is accurate. Use one space for each letter, space and punctuation mark. Corporate Kit orders Are Not Refundable.

																				*45	

State of Incorporation: <u>California</u>

☑ **Nolo Advantage Corporate Records Kit** .... $ __79.95__

OPTIONS:

☐ **Extra Stock Certificates** minimum order for $39.00 for 20 extra stock certificates, plus 50¢ for each additional certificate above this amount .... $ _____

☐ **Corporate Seal** (1-45 characters) $30.00   ☐ (*45+characters) $55.00 .... $ _____

Year of Incorporation: _____

Please note: *Corporate Seal will be shipped under separate cover.*

SUBTOTAL.. $ _____

Please add applicable sales tax .... $ _____

SHIPPING & HANDLING   ☐ $10.00 **or** ☐ $25.00 .... $ _____

Regular $10.00 shipping within 10 business days/Rush $25.00 shipping within 4 business days

TOTAL.. $ _____

Prices Are Subject to Change Without Notice.

Orders will not be processed unless paid in full. Call us for current prices before you submit your order at 1-800-728-3555.

METHOD OF PAYMENT ☐ Check enclosed   ☐ VISA   ☐ MasterCard   ☐ Discover Card   ☐ American Express

SIGNATURE _____   ACCOUNT # _____   EXP. DATE _____

NAME _____

STREET ADDRESS (NO PO BOXES) _____

CITY _____   STATE _____   ZIP _____   PHONE _____

DAYTIME PHONE NUMBER _____   E-MAIL ADDRESS _____

SORRY, WE DO NOT ACCEPT TELEPHONE ORDERS FOR CORPORATE RECORDS KITS.

Send to: CORPORATE KITS
NOLO PRESS/FOLK LAW, INC. 950 PARKER STREET, BERKELEY, CA 94710
Fax to: 800-645-0895

(Adv.Corp Records Kit—Book Elements)

THE PORTFOLIO CORPORATE RECORDS KIT

Nolo Press, in cooperation with Excelsior Legal, offers the Portfolio Corporate Records Kit. This deluxe corporate records kit features:

- **Corporate Records Binder** • The binder is hand-crafted of red and black simulated leather with your corporate name embossed in gold on the spine.
- **20 Stock Certificates** • These numbered, lithographed green and black certificates are customized with your corporation's name and state of formation. They contain the same special legend that is printed on the stock certifictaes in this book. Please see chapter 5, Step 3D for details.
- **Index Dividers** for your Articles, Bylaws, Minutes and Stock Certificates
- **Share Register, Stock Transfer Ledger** and **Minute Paper**
- **Corporate Seal** • The corporate seal is a solid metal embossing tool and although not legally requried, many corporations use it to indicate that a document is a duly authorized act of the corporation.

ORDER COUPON

The Portfolio Corporate Records Kit - CALIFORNIA WITH 5C STOCK LEGEND

Name of Corporation - Please print the corporate name exactly as it appears on your Articles making sure Capital and lower case letters are clear and the spelling is accurate. Use one space for each letter, space and punctuation mark. Corporate Kits Are Not Refundable.

*45

Year of Incorporation: _____   State of Incorporation: _____

☑ **Portfolio Corporate Records Kit** .... $ __129.95__

OPTIONS:

☐ **Extra Stock Certificates** minimum order for **$39.00** for 20 extra stock certificates, plus 50¢ for each additional certificate above this amount .... $ _____

Please indicate starting number for extra stock certificates
(if no number specified numbering starts with 21): _____

☐ **Extra Corporate Seal** (1-45 characters) $30.00   ☐ (*45+characters) $55.00 .... $ _____

SUBTOTAL .... $ _____

Please add applicable sales tax .... $ _____

SHIPPING & HANDLING   ☐ $10.00 **or**   ☐ $25.00 .... $ _____

Regular $10.00 shipping within 10 business days/Rush $25.00 shipping within 4 business days

TOTAL .... $ _____

Prices Are Subject to Change Without Notice.

Orders will not be processed unless paid in full. Call us for current prices before you submit your order at 1-800-728-3555.

METHOD OF PAYMENT   ☐ Check enclosed   ☐ VISA   ☐ MasterCard   ☐ Discover Card   ☐ American Express

SIGNATURE _____   ACCOUNT # _____   EXP. DATE _____

NAME _____

STREET ADDRESS (NO PO BOXES) _____

CITY _____   STATE _____   ZIP _____   PHONE _____

DAYTIME PHONE NUMBER _____   E-MAIL ADDRESS _____

SORRY, WE DO NOT ACCEPT TELEPHONE ORDERS FOR CORPORATE RECORDS KITS.

Send to: CORPORATE KITS
NOLO PRESS/FOLK LAW, INC. 950 PARKER STREET, BERKELEY, CA 94710
Fax to: 800-645-0895

(BLUMBERG KIT-Book Elements)

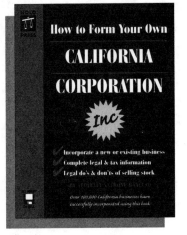

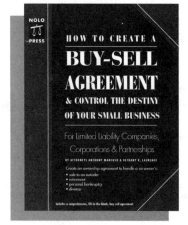
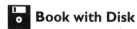
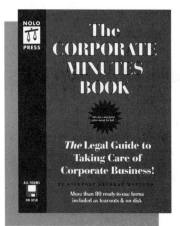

Take 2 Minutes
& Give Us Your 2 cents

Your comments make a big difference in the development and revision of Nolo books and software. Please take a few minutes and register your Nolo product—and your comments—with us. Not only will your input make a difference, you'll receive special offers available only to registered owners of Nolo products on our newest books and software. Register now by:

PHONE
1-800-992-6656

FAX
1-800-645-0895

EMAIL
cs@nolo.com

or **MAIL** us
this registration card

REMEMBER:
Little publishers have big ears. We really listen to you.

fold here

NOLO

PRESS

REGISTRATION CARD

NAME		DATE	
ADDRESS			
CITY		STATE	ZIP
PHONE		E-MAIL	

WHERE DID YOU HEAR ABOUT THIS PRODUCT?

WHERE DID YOU PURCHASE THIS PRODUCT?

DID YOU CONSULT A LAWYER? (PLEASE CIRCLE ONE)   YES   NO   NOT APPLICABLE

DID YOU FIND THIS BOOK HELPFUL?   (VERY)   5   4   3   2   1   (NOT AT ALL)

COMMENTS

WAS IT EASY TO USE?   (VERY EASY)   5   4   3   2   1   (VERY DIFFICULT)

DO YOU OWN A COMPUTER? IF SO, WHICH FORMAT? (PLEASE CIRCLE ONE)   WINDOWS   DOS   MAC

❑ If you do not wish to receive mailings from these companies, please check this box.
❑ You can quote me in future Nolo Press promotional materials. Daytime phone number _____.

QUIC 1.0

NOLO IN THE NEWS

"Nolo helps lay people perform legal tasks without the aid—or fees—of lawyers."
—USA TODAY

Nolo books are ..."written in plain language, free of legal mumbo jumbo, and spiced with witty personal observations."
—ASSOCIATED PRESS

"...Nolo publications...guide people simply through the how, when, where and why of law."
—WASHINGTON POST

"Increasingly, people who are not lawyers are performing tasks usually regarded as legal work... And consumers, using books like Nolo's, do routine legal work themselves."
—NEW YORK TIMES

"...All of [Nolo's] books are easy-to-understand, are updated regularly, provide pull-out forms...and are often quite moving in their sense of compassion for the struggles of the lay reader."
—SAN FRANCISCO CHRONICLE

fold here

NOLO PRESS
950 Parker Street
Berkeley, CA 94710-9867

PRESS **Attn:** **QUIC 1.0**